smøyg

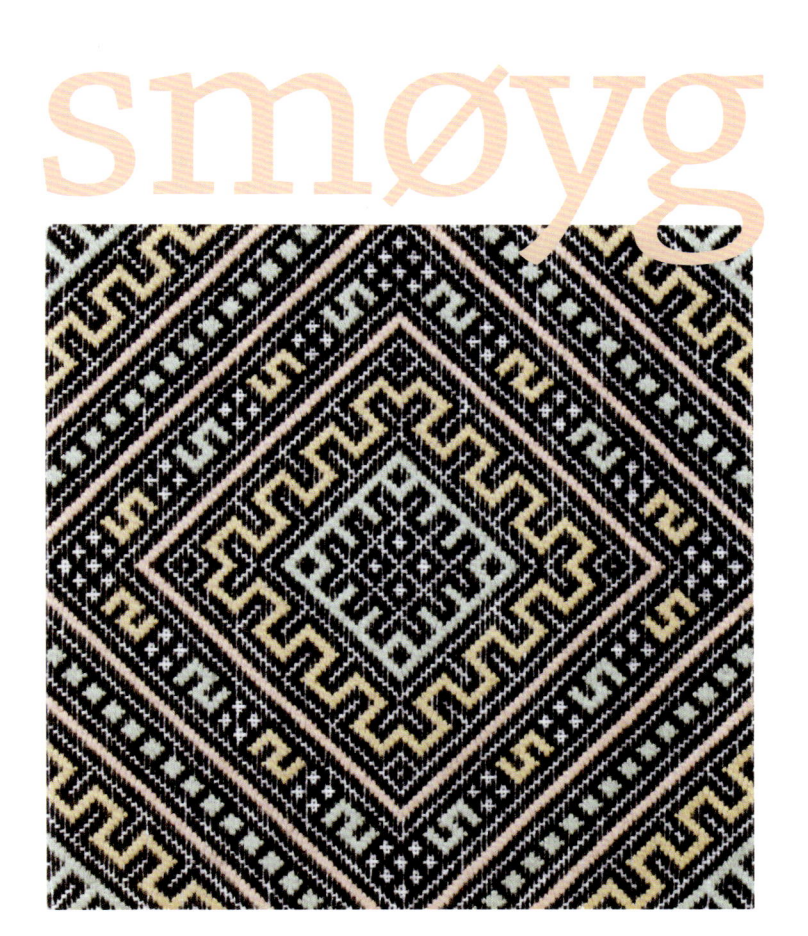

This edition published in Great Britain in 2018 by
Search Press Ltd
Wellwood
North Farm Road
Tunbridge Wells
Kent TN2 3DR
www.searchpress.com

Originally published in 2018 in Australia by
Vetty Creations
PO Box 1723, Hornsby Westfield NSW 1635, Australia

Copyright © Yvette Stanton 2018

All rights reserved. No part of this book, text, photographs or illustrations may be reproduced or transmitted in any form or by any means by print, photoprint, microfilm, microfiche, photocopier, internet or in any way known or as yet unknown, or stored in a retrieval system, without written permission obtained beforehand of the copyright holder.

ISBN: 978-1-78221-710-7

This book was conceived, designed and produced by Yvette Stanton, Vetty Creations

The Publishers and author can accept no responsibility for any consequences arising from the information, advice or instructions given in this publication. Readers are permitted to reproduce any of the items in this book for their personal use, or for the purposes of selling for charity, free of charge and without the prior permission of the Publishers. Any use of the items for commercial purposes is not permitted without the prior permission of the Publishers.

suppliers
If you have difficulty in obtaining any of the materials and equipment mentioned in this book, please visit the Search Press or Vetty Creations websites for details of suppliers: www.searchpress.com
www.vettycreations.com.au

Printed in China by Everbest Printing.

cataloguing-in-publication data
Stanton, Yvette, 1974—
 Smøyg: Pattern Darning from Norway

 104 p. : col. ill ; 28 cm
  Bibliography.
  Includes index.
  ISBN 978-1-78221-710-7

 1. Embroidery – Norway – History
 2. Embroidery – Norwegian
 3. Embroidery – Patterns
 4. Embroidery – Handbooks, manuals etc.
 5. Clothing and dress – Norway – History

746.44

acknowledgements
John Stanton, Emma and Iona, Frank and Yvonne Wilkey, Kari-Anne Pedersen, Agnete Sivertsen, Kari Bjercke, Kjersti Lyngestad, Inger Holm Jørgensen, Inger Petersen, Ingebjørg Vaagen, Liv Berit Kaasa, Aafke Buurs, Heidi Fossnes, Mary Corbet, Julie Milne, Lyndell Walker, Lucia Russo, Karen at Cottage Garden Threads.

Thank you to the museums that have allowed me to reproduce works in their collections: Norsk Folkemuseum, Hardanger og Voss Museum, Telemark Museum, Vest-Telemark Museum, Amuse Museum (Japan).

bibliography and further reading
Astrup, Edle; Engelstad, Helen; Molaug, Ragnhild B. *Sting Og Søm: I Gammelt Og Nytt Broderi*, H Aschehoug & Co, Oslo, 1943.
DigitaltMuseum, www.digitalt.museum.no
Haugen, Bjørn Sverre Hol (editor). *Norsk Bunadleksikon: Alle Norsk Bunader of Samiske Folkedrakter*. N.W. Damm and Søn, 2006.
Maurer, Phyllis. *Techniques of Ukrainian Nyzynka*, Ethnic Textile Art, Lincoln, Nebraska, undated.
Pedersen, Kari-Anne. *Folkedrakt Blir Bunad*, Cappelen Damm, 2013.
Stuland, Gudrun. *Hardangerbunaden Før og No*, Fabritius Forlagshus, 1980. Reprinted 2014 by Hordaland Husflidslag, Bergen.
Stuland, Gudrun. *Hol og Svartsaum*, Fabritius and Sønners, Oslo 1966. Reprinted 2013 by Hordaland Husflidslag, Bergen.

other books by Yvette Stanton
Early-Style Hardanger: Traditional Norwegian Whitework Embroidery
Elegant Hardanger Embroidery
Portuguese Whitework: Bullion embroidery from Guimarães
Sardinian Knotted Embroidery: Whitework from Teulada
The Left-Handed Embroiderer's Companion: a Step-by-Step Stitch Dictionary
The Right-Handed Embroiderer's Companion: a Step-by-Step Stitch Dictionary
Ukrainian Drawn Thread Embroidery: Merezhka Poltavska
With Prue Scott:
Mountmellick Embroidery: Inspired by Nature

In loving memory of Rene Wilkey who always encouraged my creativity.

smøyg

PATTERN DARNING FROM NORWAY

YVETTE STANTON

Search Press

vetty creations

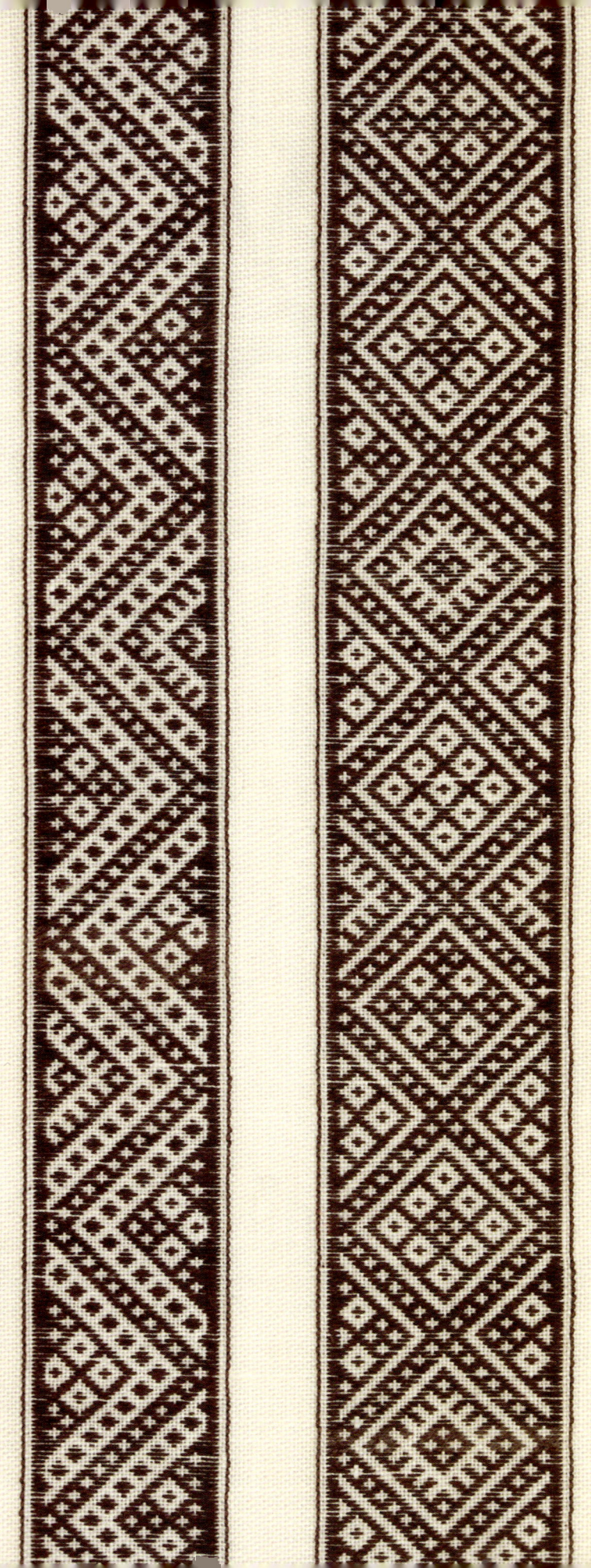

contents

What is smøyg? 5
Where is smøyg found? 6
History 7
Smøyg basics 8
Skjorte 9
Handaplagg 12
Belte 13
Likkross 14
Brudgomaduk 15
Luve/lue 16
Brystduk 18
Kinnlag 19
Skaut 20
Kasteplagg 21
Forerme 21
Forklebord 21
Motifs 22
Same design, different colours 23
Fabric 24
Thread 25
Needles 26
Projects 27
    Jewellery bag 28
    Needlecase 30
    Table runner 32
    Espresso pendant 35
    Band sampler 36
    Bookmarks 44
    Hanging ornament 46
    Table centre 47
    Poppy pendant 51
    Cushion 52
    Shirt 56
    Framed square 60
    Scissor keep 62
Stitches and techniques 65
Appendix: fabric and thread
    compatibility 100
Image credits 103
Index 104

what is smøyg?

Smøyg or smøygsaum (occasionally smöigsaum) is Norwegian pattern darning. Working with running stitch, by counting the threads of the fabric, and placing the stitches according to a graph, patterns can be created. Smøyg forms part of the decoration of traditional clothing, known as bunad, in a number of regions.

There are four main variations, to do with colour.

1. monochrome
The monochrome variation, uses black stitching on white fabric. Shown top right.

2. red with highlights
The embroidery is worked in a main colour (usually red) with highlights of a few other colours either for distinct motifs or simple stripes of colour within the main design. Shown right.

3. striped
The third variation, shown right, uses stripes of many colours across the whole design. Sometimes there is a pattern to the order of the colours. At other times, the colour placement is more random. Red is often, but not always, used for every second stripe.

4. coloured
The fourth variation, shown bottom right, uses myriad colours, often with one or two base colours, and then other colours picking out motifs.

Smøyg is pronounced as follows:

smǝaɪg
or
s – as in "salt"
m – as in "more"
ø – as in "book"
y – as in "see"
g – as in "big"

or
s – as in "salt"
m – as in "more"
øy – as in "gooey"
g – as in "big"

NF.1911-1264

NF.1921-0661

VF.09374

where is smøyg found?

Smøyg is mainly found on clothing in the south and southwest, in the regions of Aust- and Vest-Telemark (Telemark county), Setesdal (Aust-Agder county) and Hardanger (Hordaland county).

The Hardanger vinterbunad has black smøyg cuffs, collar and front yoke on the shirt, and a border across the apron bottom. See pages 11 and 21.

Hardanger bridegrooms may carry a handkerchief with svartsaum (black embroidery) including smøyg. See page 15.

From Hardanger, a bib worn on the chest, is known as a brystduk. See page 18.

Belts in Hardanger feature red smøyg with highlights. See page 13.

Hardanger bride shirt with black smøyg cuffs, collar and front yoke. See page 11.

In Hardanger, the handaplagg – a cloth for women to cover their hands – is worked in svartsaum including smøyg. See page 12.

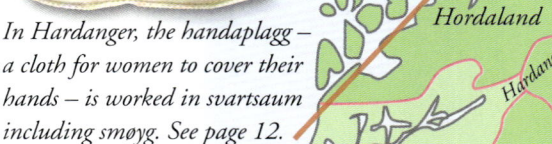

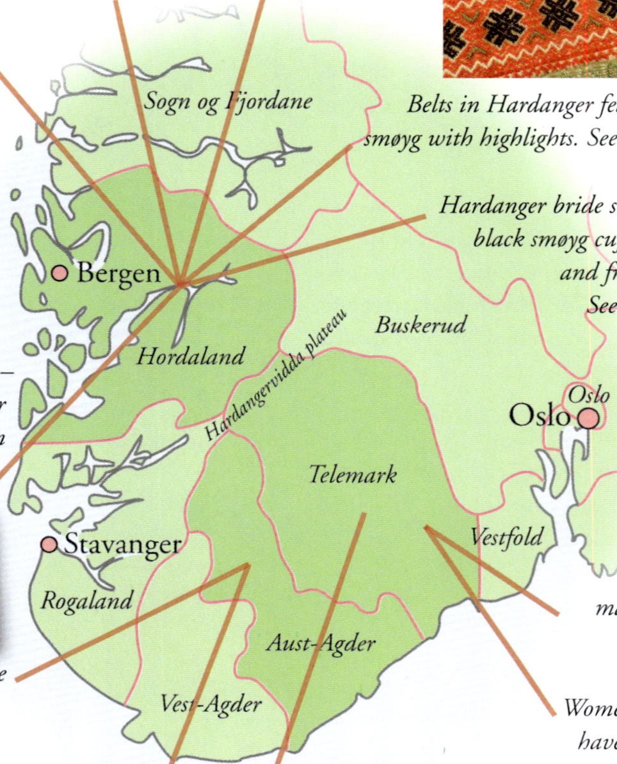

Aust-Telemark bridegrooms may carry a handkerchief with striped smøyg. See page 15.

In Setesdal, baby wraps feature striped smøyg and red smøyg with highlights. See page 19.

Women's bunad shirts in Telemark have coloured smøyg collars (and sometimes cuffs). See pages 9–10.

Caps for young children in Setesdal and Vest-Telemark have red smøyg with highlights, and ties with striped smøyg. See pages 16–17.

Ceremonial cloths known as likkross, come from Telemark. They usually feature a number of monochrome or striped bands of smøyg at either end of the long cloth. See page 14.

6

history

Smøyg is said to date from Viking times (late 700s through to 1000s). It probably came to Norway with the Vikings, or through trade. The oldest example of smøyg embroidery in Norway dates from the 1400s.

Most of the smøyg found in Norway is in the south and south western counties, particularly in Hordaland, Telemark and Aust-Agder. Roads are scarce between these counties as there is a large highland plateau, the Hardangervidda, bordering the north of Telemark, which would make travel difficult during wintery times. However, it is likely that the embroidery spread along trade routes a long time ago, and then over time the technique was absorbed into the local clothing styles, and expressed in unique ways for each region.

Smøyg can be found in small quantities on clothing in other regions, however, these would be exceptions rather than the rule. For example, in Hallingdal in Buskerud county, smøyg can sometimes be found on collars and cuffs of shirts. Some can be found on garments in Sogn og Fjordane. These are both adjacent counties to either Hordaland or Telemark. What is surprising is that there seem to be few or no examples of smøyg in Rogaland and Vest-Agder, counties which are also adjacent, to the south.

While women's clothing is well documented, men's traditional clothing is less so. Some of the shirts, collars or cuffs in museums are highly likely to be men's clothing, but are not always recorded as such.

As pattern darning uses one of the most simple stitches – running stitch – it is a technique that has been used in many cultures. In Japan it is known as *kogin* or *koginzashi*. In Ukraine it is known as *nyzynka*, and in Sweden it is known as *vävsöm*, which translates to woven stitching. We also see pattern darning in European darning samplers from 1700–1800s, and Mamluk darning samplers from Egypt in the period of 1200–1500.

Detail of jacket with kogin embroidery, from Tsugaru in Aomori prefecture, Japan.

Danish darning sampler, circa 1815. Silk on muslin.

14th–15th century Mamluk sampler, Egypt. The sampler has several bands of pattern darning in the top left corner.

smøyg basics

The main stitch used in pattern darning is running stitch. There are also small amounts of satin stitch used, but these are only occasional. Most smøyg features only running stitch.

The stitching is usually worked across the shortest distance of the pattern, so that the lines are short lines rather than long lines. For a design which is one long band, the whole design is usually worked from side to side across the short dimension. Occasionally one can find an example where the design is worked along the length of the design, or small elements at the side are worked across the opposite dimension. Even more rarely, one can find a design that has different parts stitched across different dimensions.

When the stitching is worked along the length, it may be that it is not actually stitched. Weaving methods have been created to manufacture cloth which looks like smøyg but where the pattern is created as part of the weaving process. Some of the modern bunads feature this work as it is much cheaper to produce as the process is mechanised.

Most smøyg is worked on a single layer of fabric, however, some collars use double thickness, sewing through one or both layers depending on which stitch is being used. The double thickness would have been for strength (collars receive a lot of wear and tear) and stiffness.

The following pages show the main applications and styles of smøyg found on clothing and textiles in Norway.

This shirt from Hardanger in Hordaland, dating from the early 1800s, uses running stitch smøyg and cross stitch.

The collar of a shirt from Heddal in Telemark, featuring coloured smøyg. The first or base layer is worked with dark brown and orange sections. Additional colour of red, light browns and yellows, is added on the second or top layer.

This baby's cap from Setesdal in Aust-Agder, is primarily worked in lines across the design. However, at the edges, the triangle shapes have lines worked down the design.

This bride's handcloth, dated 1806, from Sauherad in Telemark, is stitched in faded silk on linen. The band shown has stitching along the length of the band rather than the usual short lines across the band.

skjorte

A skjorte is a shirt. Across Norway, bunad shirts feature many different styles of embroidery. The main two regions that feature smøyg on their shirts are Telemark and Hardanger. Other regions may sometimes have smøyg on their shirts, but these are more likely to be variations on or exceptions to the regular style.

telemark skjorte

In Telemark, the embroidery is usually worked in full colour, and can feature on the shirt collar (*kvarde*), cuffs, or front yoke. The largest range of historical examples remaining are collars, as these most commonly featured smøyg.

Traditionally the shirts featured a number of different styles of embroidery, and many different colours. Therefore, smøyg is usually used in combination with other embroideries, such as plattsøm (satin stitch) in rosemaling style, drawn thread work, and other counted embroidery styles. By using many styles and colours the shirts make more of a visual impact. It would not be usual to find smøyg on the collar, cuffs and yoke of one shirt.

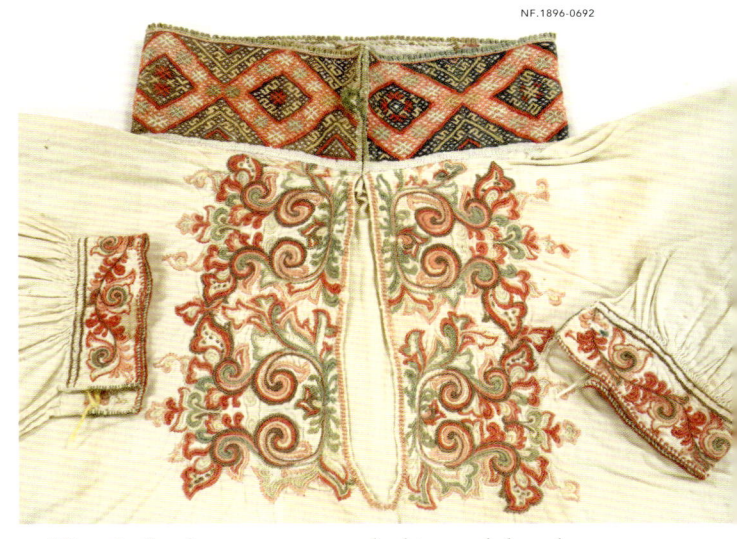

Historically, the smøyg was worked in wool thread on linen or sometimes on cotton fabric. The embroidered fabric usually had between 40 and 55 threads per inch (16–22 threads per cm). Some historical shirts are worked in silk thread, but this is less common than wool. Most stitchers now work their smøyg (these garments are still made and worn) in cotton thread, probably because wool thread that is fine enough can be difficult to obtain.

The shirts feature colours such as red, orange, brown, green, and black. Blue, pink and purple are not common, however, when synthetic dyes were introduced, colour-schemes often became much brighter and stronger.

Right: this shirt from Telemark has smøyg in two places: on the collar, and multicoloured stripe near the top edge of the sleeve cuff. The collar (detail above) is worked in very fine, wool on linen of about 55 count. The wool used on the cuff (detail below) appears to be quite fluffy, due to the way the smøyg edges are worked.

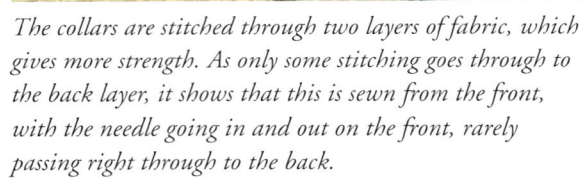

The collars are stitched through two layers of fabric, which gives more strength. As only some stitching goes through to the back layer, it shows that this is sewn from the front, with the needle going in and out on the front, rarely passing right through to the back.

hardanger skjorte

In Hardanger, smøyg is worked in black on the shirts of Hardanger *vinterbunaden* (winterbunads), on bridal shirts, and on the *forklebord* (apron band). Unlike regular Hardanger bunads, vinterbunaden usually feature no Hardanger embroidery at all. Instead they have smøyg.

The smøyg is worked in black silk, on linen or cotton fabric. Sometimes the silk is flat or filament silk with a very slight twist. At other times the silk is plied and more highly twisted, like the appearance of a pearl cotton. On many of the older examples, the black silk thread has faded to brown, and even started to rot.

The embroidery is worked on the collar, down either side of the front yoke opening, and the sleeve cuffs. The embroidery on the yoke opening is often finer than the collar embroidery, with fabric of up to 60 count.

The designs often feature a diamond framework with various motifs such as the åttebladrose (the eight-pointed "star" shape), eldjarnrose, and zig-zags.

11

handaplagg

These are cloths which are used to cover the hands, for modesty. They were used by women for church, and by brides at weddings.

The example shown right, NF.1911-0008, is worked in silk thread on linen fabric. It dates from before 1911. When silk thread is old, it can rot and fade. This one shows some signs of rotting, with the missing border at top left, and also fading with the stripes across some of the motifs. The handaplagg features cross stitch and smøyg. Most of the design is worked in cross stitch, with the large, densely worked, diamond-shaped motifs in smøyg. Each of these motifs is worked with the running stitch lying horizontally, except for the two diamonds on the left and right of the central diamond. These two motifs are worked with vertical stitching lines.

As these cloths are often used by brides, it is not unreasonable to expect that the motifs used would be associated with fertility.

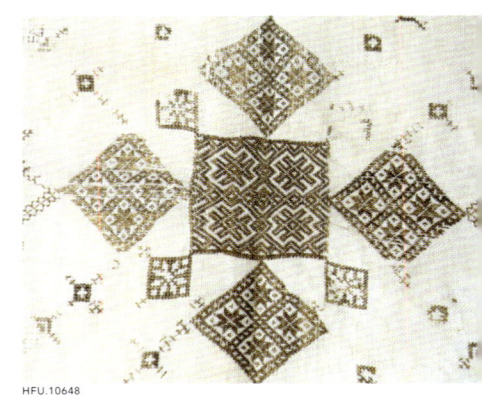

NF.1911-0008

NF.1911-0008

HFU.10648

HFU.10648

HFU.347

belte

Belts from the Hardanger region are worn over the bottom of the waistcoat, and the top of the skirt and apron. The smøyg is worked on linen of about 40 count, with wool yarn. Later examples are worked in cotton on linen. They are worked predominantly in red, with highlights of other colours such as green, yellow and black.

The belts are usually edged in silk ribbon. Some belts have lapbands that hang over the apron, as shown right.

BUM.2059

HFU.18368

HFU.675

HFU.1177

HFU.18370

HFU.352

HFU.177

HFU.2385

HFU.18463

BUM.2055

NF.2000-1699

BUM.2047

likkross

A likkross is a ceremonial textile, of which one use is being laid upon the coffin for a funeral.

Likkross cloths are rectangular in shape. At the ends of the cloth, there are usually bands of embroidery, and these are where smøyg is most often found. There are two main styles of these cloths, both from Telemark. Each style has bands of smøyg interspersed with bands of holbeinsøm, which is two-coloured double running stitch. They usually have large motifs in the centre section, often cross stitch and holbeinsøm, with tassels hanging off the corners of the cloth.

The first style, left, which dates from around the 1780s onwards, has bands of striping smøyg, worked in wool. The stripes change colour regularly or irregularly. Colours used are most often blue and green interspersed between red stripes. The end of row turns are usually on the front.

The second style, below, usually worked on 32–36 count linen, has bands of black or brown silk smøyg featuring diamonds or, unusually zig-zags. Zig-zags are not a common motif in smøyg, with diamonds much more prevalent. The end of row turns are usually on the front.

Left and above left: This style of likkross comes from the Aust- and Midt-Telemark regions. This particular example is worked on approximately 57 count linen, with wool in cross stitch, holbein stitch and smøyg.

Left and above: This style of likkross from Notodden in Aust-Telemark, dates from circa 1880. The smøyg bands were worked in black or brown silk. It is difficult to know whether the brown has faded from black, or was always brown. The band above shows the lines of stitching going along the band, which is not usual.

brudgomaduk

Brudgomaduken, which translates to bride groom cloths, are a handkerchief-like cloth used as part of bridal attire, usually hanging off the groom's clothing in a decorative manner.

Telemark-style cloths, shown right, are around 20 x 30 cm (8 x 12 in), with wide borders of smøyg, in striped colouring. There are separate motifs – usually fancy cross shapes – in the centre, which are also worked in striped smøyg. The yarn is wool, on linen fabric. They may have tassels hanging off two or more corners.

In the Hardanger region, with examples shown below and right, the brudgomaduken are more usually square, and worked in black silk on white linen fabric. They feature large motifs in the corners and centre, some with smaller motifs filling the spaces between. The motifs are worked in cross stitch and holbein stitch, with the centres of the large motifs most often worked in smøyg. The cloth's corners sometimes have coloured tassels.

15

luve/lue

Infant cap from Setesdal and Vest-Telemark.
Also known as dreglehuve, dåpslue.

These caps are worn by babies and infants up to about the age of three. They were used from at least the 1800s onwards, and are still used today, mainly for ceremonial purposes such as christenings.

The smøyg motifs are decorative and some also believe they offer protection to the child. The semi-circular section is worn at the front, with the wide rectangular section covering the skull. There is usually a band which wraps around the head to keep the cap in place.

The embroidery on the main part of the cap is usually worked predominantly in red. On some caps there are specific motifs worked in other colours. On others there are narrow stripes across the design worked in alternate colours. Other caps have elements of the borders worked in alternate colours.

Sometimes the design has a central panel with borders on either side. Some have all over patterns.

The embroidery on the band is treated differently. It is a narrow band of pattern, repeating along the length of the band. It is usually worked in stripes with red alternating with other colours e.g. red, green, red, black, red, green, red, black.

The embroidery on these caps is usually worked in wool yarn on linen or cotton fabric.

Left & above left: This cap features a central design with side borders. The wool yarn uses synthetic dyes.
Below & below left: This cap features very fine embroidery on fine linen. The yarn uses natural dyes.

NF.1955-0492

NF.1968-0637

NF.1955-0492

NF.1968-0637

NF.1949-0525

NF.1911-1264

LB.06130

FYB.00096

FYB.00100

FYB.00100

17

brystduk

Breast cloth from the Hardanger region. Also known as bringeduk, bringklut and brystklut.

These cloths are worn on the chest over the shirt, under the waistcoat. The smøyg is predominantly red. Some cloths have all over designs, and others have stripes, which can be straight or zig-zagging.

Wool yarn is used on linen or cotton fabric, of about 40 count.

Older cloths use natural dyes and have less vibrant colours. More recent examples use synthetic dyes which tend to be brighter.

NF.1992-2156

Designs feature horizontal bands, zig-zagging, or all over designs.

HFU.00028

BUM.0754

BG.00251

HFU.17926

BUM.1070

BUM.1059

BUM.1008

HFU.00052

18

kinnlag

These cloths, also known as kinnplagg, hyllik and hylk, were used for swaddling babies.

These linen cloths were wrapped around babies in a shawl-like manner. In the late 1800s they were for daily use, and later just for baptisms.

In Setesdal in Aust-Agder, red wool was the predominant embroidery fibre, with individual motifs picked out in other colours such as brown, black, green and blue. The long, narrow cloths usually had a border along one side or both, with the border in stripes.

The baby would wear a cap (*lue*) embroidered with smøyg. The cloth was draped over the head (with face still showing), and then wrapped down over the body. Woven straps were then wrapped around to hold it all together.

In Hordaland, the cloths were more square, and featured a section of lace along one side. Next to the lace would be a band of black smøyg, worked in silk. Sometimes this band would instead be worked in cross stitch, but with some accompanying large smøyg motifs further towards the middle of the cloth.

*Above right: Three kinnlag cloths from Valle, in Setesdal, Aust-Agder. The top two feature motifs such as kinnekross and hakekross. The one at the bottom is a less typical design.
Right: Detail of hyllik from Hordaland, featuring three large smøyg motifs, with cross stitched motifs*

Left: This hyllik from Hordaland shows how they were worn under the baby's cap.

A note on the use of the hakekross

The swastika symbol, which in Norway is known as the *hakekross* (meaning hooked cross), has been used in many cultures and possibly dates back to 13000 BC in eastern Europe. For many it has come to have very negative connotations. Its inclusion in this book is as part of the historical record and is not intended to offend. It is not used in any of the projects.

skaut

A skaut is a headdress, worn by married women for modesty. In Voss they feature svartsaum (blackwork), in cross stitch and holbein stitch. Very occasionally a skaut from Voss may feature smøyg as part of the design.

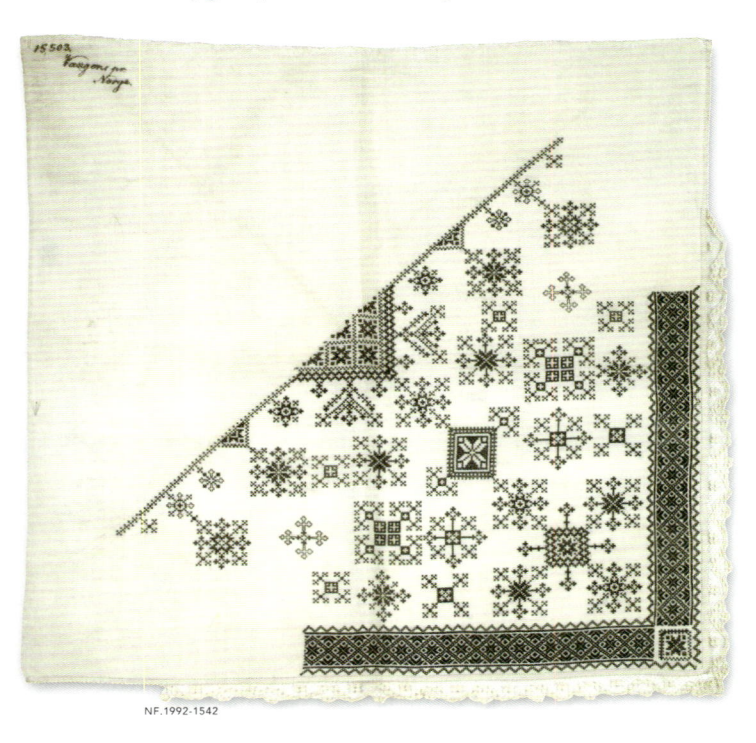

On the skaut shown left and below, and as with many examples from Voss, the majority of the stitching is in cross stitch with small quantities of holbein stitch. The border along the edge is worked in smøyg, using black silk thread. This skaut dates from before 1877.

Headdresses from Voss are worn over a padded board which helps to create the triangular shape.

kasteplagg

A kasteplagg is bridal clothing, worn over the bride's headdress. From Aust-Telemark.

While mostly stitched in cross stitch and holbeinsøm, sometimes kasteplagg cloths feature small motifs of smøyg. The smøyg is usually worked in red, blue and yellow. The example shows very fluffy wool used for the smøyg, which probably came from the Norwegian spælsau sheep.

forerme

These cuffs known as forerme, from the Hardanger region, are worn under a jacket with just the pretty part peeking out from the end of the sleeve.

Forerme often use short versions of smøyg designs that feature on belts. They are usually worked predominantly in red wool, with highlights in other colours.

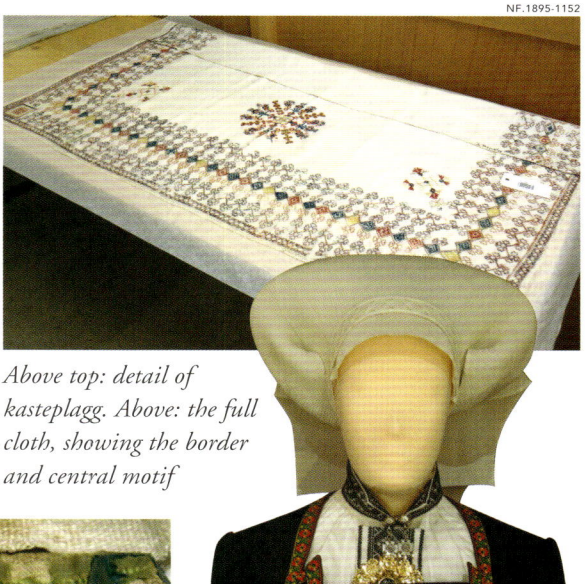

forklebord

The Hardanger vinterbunad (winter bunad) has a black apron (forkle) instead of the usual white one. The white apron features Hardanger, whereas the black apron features a band (forklebord) of smøyg.

The embroidery is worked in black silk (or cotton more contemporarily), in intricate designs.

Above top: detail of kasteplagg. Above: the full cloth, showing the border and central motif

Above: two examples of cuffs, showing variations on the one design.

Right: Hardanger vinterbunad with forklebord on the apron.

21

motifs

Traditional motifs' names can vary depending on regional dialects.

kinnekross, eldjarnrose | *kinnekross, eldjarnrose* | crosses

hakekross | *åttebladrose* – Telemark style | *åttebladrose* – Hordaland style

ship, twin ships | *chi monogram* | *essesaum* (s stitching)

valknute – Hordaland style | *valknute* – Telemark style | *spissruter, mæander-ruter* (meandering lines)

other motifs

Combinations of other motifs, and those without common names.

same design, different colours

There are some designs that turn up again and again, interpreted in different colour schemes. The colours, and their placement, can make a significant difference to how the design looks.

The images in each column have the same design (sometimes with minor variations), interpreted in different ways by varying the colours and their placement.

TGM-SM.0711

NF.1912-0338

NF.1992-2484

TGM-SM.0876

NF.1904-0181

NF.1992-2485

TGM-SM.0716

NF.1913-1298

NF.1910-0987

TGM-SM.0719

NF.1912-0345

NF.1912-0489

TGM-SM.0715

NF.1992-2569

TGM-SM.0721

TGM-SM.0712

TGM-SM.2542

TGM-SM.0722

TGM-BM.1933-34:048

TGM-SM.0890

fabric

The fabric used for smøyg was white (or offwhite) linen or cotton fabric. Originally only linen would have been used. However, from the 1800s onwards, cotton fabric became just as commonly used.

Evenweave fabric has the same number of threads over the same distance across both dimensions of the fabric. It does not refer to whether the fabric has any slubs or not. For some types of embroidery it is important to have fabric that is evenweave, as the design will turn out in a predictable manner, such as squares turning out square. While this is advantageous for smøyg, it is not absolutely essential. If a fabric is not evenweave, it just means that shapes will be more squashed in one direction than the other.

Thread count, or fabric count, is the number of threads per inch, and can differ between the warp (down the length of the fabric) and weft (across the fabric, from side to side, or selvedge to selvedge).

The fabric used for some smøyg applications was extremely fine. Smøyg on some shirts from both Telemark and Hardanger was on up to 60 count fabric (24 threads per cm). When this was the case, the other parts of the garment were more likely to be made of a more coarse, lower count linen. Other items including belts and breast cloths, used lower counts of fabric, such as 40 count (16 threads per cm).

Flax grew in Norway, and therefore linen could be home grown and woven. Cotton was not a crop that grew well in Norway, and therefore cotton was originally not so commonly used. Cotton had advantages over linen that made it preferable, though it was probably much more expensive to obtain.

Linen slubs, while often regarded as part of the beauty of linen, are not helpful when pattern darning. The thicker sections of fabric thread push the stitches further apart, interrupting the pattern. Every effort should be made to use linen that has threads that are as uniform in thickness as possible. However, most often slubs just have to be accepted and worked with.

Zweigart Meldal fabric, 100% cotton, 56ct/22tpc. Very uniform weave.

Weddigen 22 fabric, 100% linen, 50ct/20tpc. Slubs very noticeable.

Cotton fabric lacks the slubs of linen, and therefore has a more uniform weave. This is its main advantage over linen. Unfortunately 100% cotton evenweave fabric at appropriate counts is not commonly available.

The linen was usually bleached white, though there are many examples where the linen has since discoloured with use. Some was possibly not white to start with but more a natural coloured linen.

to prewash or not?

When fabrics are washed for the first time, they often shrink a little. Different fibres shrink different amounts. Generally speaking, linen is likely to shrink the least, cotton and silk a little more, and even more so with wool. While linen is the least likely to shrink, it is likely that it will shrink a little.

Fabric often does not shrink the same amount across the warp and weft. During the weaving process, more stress is placed on the warp threads (the ones that run down the length of the fabric) than on the weft threads (the ones that go from selvedge to selvedge). When a fabric is washed, the threads are able to relax from their stressed position. Because the warp threads are more stressed, they will often shrink a little more than the weft. Shrinkage probably will not be much: it is usually between four to seven percent.

Shrinkage could cause some problems if you've stitched on un-shrunk fabric, and then washed it later. If the amount of shrinkage was the same for both the warp and the weft, it would probably matter less, but as it can be different across both dimensions, it could make things go out of shape and pucker strangely. This is why we always pre-wash dressmaking fabric – we don't want our clothes to fit us badly!

For items that will be washed during general use, such as table linen and clothing, it makes sense to pre-wash all linen fabric, so that the fabric and fibres are stabilised back to their unstressed state before you stitch on them.

To prewash fabric, place it in cold water, and preferably leave it to soak for an hour or two. Some people advocate following this with a boiling hot water wash, another cold water wash, another boiling hot water wash, finishing with a cold wash. To dry the fabric, spin out the excess water in the washing machine's spin cycle or lay it on a thick towel, and press out the excess water. Iron the fabric to remove any wrinkles, then leave to air dry.

determining thread count of a fabric

Usually thread count is measured across an inch of fabric, even in places where inches are not used as a unit of measurement. If you don't have ruler or measuring tape showing inch measurements, 2.5 cm is approximately equal to 1 inch, and can be used instead.

To determine the thread count of a fabric, use the following method:

1 Insert a pin anywhere in the fabric.
2 Using a ruler or tape measure, measure 1 inch (2.5 cm) from the pin, in line with the threads of the fabric. At the end of the 1 inch (2.5 cm) measurement, insert another pin into the fabric. Do this along both the warp (up and down the length of the fabric) and the weft (left and right across the fabric, from selvedge to selvedge) from the original pin.
3 Count the threads between the original pin and the second pin. If there are 38 threads, then it has a thread count of 38. If there are 25 threads, the fabric is 25 count.
4 Count the threads between the original pin and the third pin. You will learn the thread count for the second dimension of the fabric.

If the two numbers are the same, the fabric is evenweave. A square design worked on evenweave fabric will turn out square. If the two numbers differ only by one or two, the fabric is nearly evenweave. A square design on such fabric will turn out nearly square. If the two numbers are markedly different, the fabric is not evenweave. A square design worked on such fabric will not turn out square. The larger a design, the more pronounced the difference will be because every additional inch expands or contracts the total quantity of threads. The difference is magnified over a large distance.

thread

The thread used for smøyg depends very much on which tradition and region it comes from. The most common types of thread used are wool, silk and cotton. Earlier examples of smøyg used wool or silk, and during the 1800s, when it started to be mass produced, cotton started to be used.

silk

One of the main ways that smøyg is used as part of the traditional costumes of Hordaland, in Hardanger and Voss predominantly, is in *svartsaum* which is blackwork (*svart* means black, and *saum* means seam, or stitching). This style of work features black stitching on white fabric. Svartsaum is usually mostly cross stitch and *holbeinsaum*

Black svartsaum showing tightly twisted silk thread.

Svartsaum that has faded to brown, showing slightly twisted flat silk.

(double running stitch) with motifs of smøyg. Svartsaum was also called *silksaum* in times past, as it was originally stitched in black silk.

Over time, on some of the historical examples, the black silk has faded to brown and either rotted or worn from use to become very thin. During the 1800s when cotton started to be mass produced, it started to be used instead of silk. In Hordaland now, cotton is used most often used for svartsaum smøyg.

Most of the silk thread had a tight twist, not unlike pearl cotton, however, some silk thread was more like flat silk with only a slight twist. When using silk, use shorter rather than longer lengths as this will stop wear and tear showing on the threads.

There are some examples of smøyg worked in silk thread in Telemark region, but these are not particularly common. Wool is much more commonly used in Telemark for smøyg.

wool

Wool thread, known as *ull* (wool) or *ullgarn* (wool yarn) in Norway, is the other main thread fibre used. Because of the fine count of fabric typically used, the wool yarn was usually much finer than crewel or lace weight yarn. Such wools are quite difficult to source these days.

Most wool in Norway would have come from spælsau sheep, which are regarded as Norway's oldest sheep breed. As well as often having quite a lustre, it could be quite a

Spælsau yarn was often used for woollen smøyg.

fluffy wool, depending the part of the sheep that the wool came from. Some of the wool was much more smooth, and tightly twisted.

When using wool for embroidery, limit the length you use to about 50 cm (20 in). Anything longer than that wears too much as it passes through the fabric repeatedly.

cotton

Most contemporary smøyg is worked in cotton thread, probably because it is now the easiest fibre to source in Norway. However, cotton was not often used traditionally, other than as a fabric to work on. There are few examples of old pieces worked in cotton thread.

dyes

Originally the wool and silk yarn would have been dyed using natural dyes, as they were the only type available.

Many of the examples before that time use reds which are orange-based reds, and a variety of other colours, such as oranges, browns, and greens, often in quite muted tones. Black was also used.

Later, aniline dyes were used, bringing an expanded colour range particularly to the shirts of Telemark bunads. The reds are stronger and sometimes bluer, and brighter greens, blues, pinks and even purples are used.

Some synthetic dyes have not aged well. Shown top right of this page is a collar. The front (shown top right) is in muted creams, greys and greens, with black. However, on the back (shown middle right) apart from the black, which stayed strong and true, some of the colours used to be quite different. The purple has faded to grey, blue has faded to green, brown has faded to yellow, and pink has faded to cream. The example at the bottom shows a simulation of the possible original colours.

Natural dyes shown left, synthetic dyes on right.

needles

The main needles used for smøyg are tapestry needles which have a large eye and a rounded tip. The rounded tip means that they more easily pass between the fabric threads, rather than accidentally catching them or splitting them.

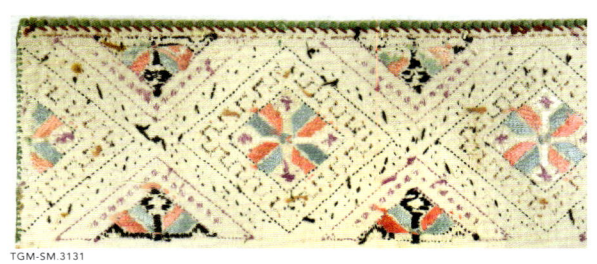

A collar from Sauherad in Telemark, from before 1890.

When working the top layer of running stitch in smøyg, a chenille needle is an advantage. Often the base layer of stitches continue behind where the second layer of stitches sit. It is best to use a chenille needle to come up through the base layer, deliberately splitting the stitches. When using a tapestry needle, the needle would be more likely to slip beside the previous stitches, causing them to sit crooked or out of line.

A chenille needle with the same number as a tapestry needle is the same length and thickness as the tapestry, but it has a sharp point instead of a rounded one.

When choosing a needle, my preference is for a larger needle, rather than a smaller one. The needle's purpose is to create a hole in the fabric through which the thread can pass easily. As a needle actually carries the doubled thread (the working thread and its tail) through the fabric at its eye, the needle should be at least as thick as, or thicker than the doubled thread. Anything thinner will cause the thread to be subjected to excess wear and tear.

For wool thread, because of the natural "fuzz" of the thread, the needle should account for the fuzz. If it does not, the thread will wear out more quickly.

Many people choose a needle based on how small and dainty it feels in their hand. However, if the needle is too small for the thread you are using, you are doing yourself a disservice. Choose your needle based on the thickness of the thread rather than the size you are used to.

projects

jewellery bag

Use this jewellery bag for a smøyg pendant necklace. The white tooth edging at the top of the bag was traditionally used on shirts in the Hardanger region, along the edge of the smøyg collar. If using 50 count fabric scares you, you could scale it up to a larger count with a thicker thread, and make it into a lingerie bag.

size of the bag 6.8 x 11.8 cm / 2 11/16 x 4 5/8 in
design thread dimensions 106 (w) x 107 (h) threads
materials and equipment
- 25 x 20 cm (10 x 8 in) 50 count linen, white
- 1 skein Au Ver à Soie, Soie d'Alger, 4106
- 1 reel Londonderry linen 100/3, white
- No 26 tapestry needle
- 70 cm (27 ½ in) narrow ribbon to tie the bag, white
- 12.5 cm (5 in) hoop
- machine-sewing thread, white and a pale colour

embroidery

❶ *Follow the chart for stitch placement.*

1 From the bottom right corner of the linen, measure across 5.5 cm (2 3/16 in). From this point, measure up 7.5 cm (2 15/16 in). Start stitching the right corner at this point.
2 Mount the fabric in a hoop so that it is drum tight.
3 Work the design in running stitch using one strand of the black silk thread.

tooth edging and construction

1 With the embroidery in the bottom right corner, count out 20 threads from the left, bottom and right corners of the diamond. Using the pale coloured machine-sewing thread, run a line of tacking across the fabric at each of these points.

2 Count 110 threads up from the top corner of the embroidery. Withdraw the next 10 thread across the width of the fabric.

❶ *This creates the area for the tooth edging.*

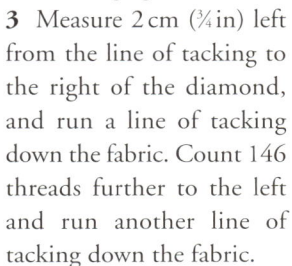

3 Measure 2 cm (¾ in) left from the line of tacking to the right of the diamond, and run a line of tacking down the fabric. Count 146 threads further to the left and run another line of tacking down the fabric.

❶ *This creates two panels; the embroidered front and the back.*

4 Working in the tooth edging area in the panel with the embroidery, skip the first thread inside the tacked line.

5 Using the linen thread, work the woven bars for a tooth edging, weaving in groups of four threads, with a total of eight threads for each bar.

❶ *The bars should finish one thread before the panel's far side.*

6 Work similarly for the other panel, starting and finishing one thread inside the tacked guides.

7 Cut the fabric in two between the middle two tacked lines. Trim the fabric outside the tacked guides to 1 cm (⅜ in).

8 Trim the ends without tacking to 4 cm (1¹⁄₁₆ in) from the woven bars.

9 Zig-zag, serge or overlock the edges of the fabric.

10 With right sides together, carefully match the tacked lines. Baste the front and back panels together.

11 With an open fronted machine-sewing foot, carefully sew around the bag, precisely one thread inside the tacked guides. On the first side, stop when you get to the woven bars and start again on the other side of the woven bars. Sew for another 2 cm (¾ in), then stop. Leave a gap of 7 mm (¼ in), then sew again. On the opposite side, sew up 9 cm (3⁹⁄₁₆ in), leave a gap of 7 mm (¼ in), sew another 2 cm (¾ in), then leave a gap for the woven bars, then sew again to the top.

❶ *Finish the thread ends neatly at the end of each section.*

12 Neatly cut and remove all the unwoven threads at the drawn thread area ends, right back to the fabric edges.

13 Remove all the tacking around the edges of the bag.

14 Open the seams out flat. Fold the top of the bag down, along the middle of the woven bars. Work the first line only of kvalesaum (the backstitch part), grouping the threads in groups of four.

15 Fold 9 mm (⅜ in) to the inside at the raw top of the bag.

16 Fold everything from above the tooth edging down into the bag.

17 From the lower edge of the lower gap in the side seam on one side, backstitch across the bag (stitch length of four threads), catching the hem at the back to create the lower edge of the casing for the ribbons.

18 From the upper edge of the gap, backstitch across the bag (stitch length of four threads), again catching the hem at the back to create the upper edge of the casing for the ribbons.

19 Cut the ribbon in half. Thread one ribbon into the entire casing from one side. Thread the other from the other side. Knot the paired ribbon ends together on each side.

20 To close the bag, pull the ribbons on each side.

needlecase

This pretty needlecase features smøyg on the front and back. There are small areas of silk highlights as are occasionally found on old pieces.

size 13 x 7 cm / 5 1/8 x 2 3/4 in
design thread dimensions 198 (w) x 201 (h) threads
materials and equipment

- 30 x 30 cm (12 x 12 in) 40 count linen, cream
- Fine d'Aubusson wool, 1 skein each: 2133, 2926, 2952, 4622, 4623
- 1 reel Au Ver à Soie, Soie Perlée 080
- No 24 tapestry needle
- No 24 chenille needle
- No 9 embroidery needle
- 20 cm (8 in) hoop
- 14.4 x 15 cm (5 11/16 x 5 15/16 in) cotton backing fabric
- 11 x 12 cm (4 5/16 x 4 3/4 in) doctor's flannel, cream
- 60 cm (24 in) Lady Dot Creates cotton chenille, Barn Door
- 8 mm (5/16 in) diameter pearl button, cream
- machine-sewing thread to match fabric, and chenille

embroidery

❶ *Follow the chart for stitch and colour placement.*

1 From the top left corner of the linen, measure across 7.5 cm (3 in). From this point, measure down 7.5 cm (3 in). Start stitching the right corner at this point.
2 Mount the fabric in a hoop so that it is drum tight.
3 Work the light green sections of pattern darning: work the top, the middle and the bottom sections separately.
4 Work the light pink diagonal lines: divide the pink in two, and work the top half, then the bottom half.
5 Work the maroon centre sections.

6 Work the dark green in using the chenille needle.
7 Work the darker pink using the chenille needle.
8 Work the stone Vs and centre diamonds using the silk in the chenille needle.
9 Work the wide stem stitch using the darker pink and the chenille needle.

construction

1 Trim the fabric around the embroidery to 1cm (⅜in).
2 With right sides together, pin the embroidery to the backing fabric.
3 With the embroidered panel up, carefully machine sew around the fabric, adjacent to the edge of the embroidery, leaving a 5cm (2in) gap in one side.
4 Clip the corners and turn the needlecase the right way out through the gap. Neatly stitch the gap closed. Press.
5 Centre the doctor's flannel over the inside of the needlecase. Pin or baste it in place.
6 Turn over to the right side, and carefully machine sew down the spine of the needlecase with a 1mm (¹⁄₁₆in) wide zig-zag, in the gap between the front and back embroidery.
7 Using the embroidery needle, sew the chenille trim around the edge of the needlecase with the matching machine-sewing thread. Take 6–8mm (¼–⁵⁄₁₆in) long stitches through the fabric at the edge, alternating stitches through the linen and the backing fabric to couch the chenille. At the centre of one of the long sides, work a loop to snugly fit around the button. When the end meets the beginning, overlap the ends by about 1cm (⅜in).
8 Sew the button over the chenille trim on the opposite side, opposite the loop.
9 Remove any basting.
10 Put the button through the loop to close the needlecase.

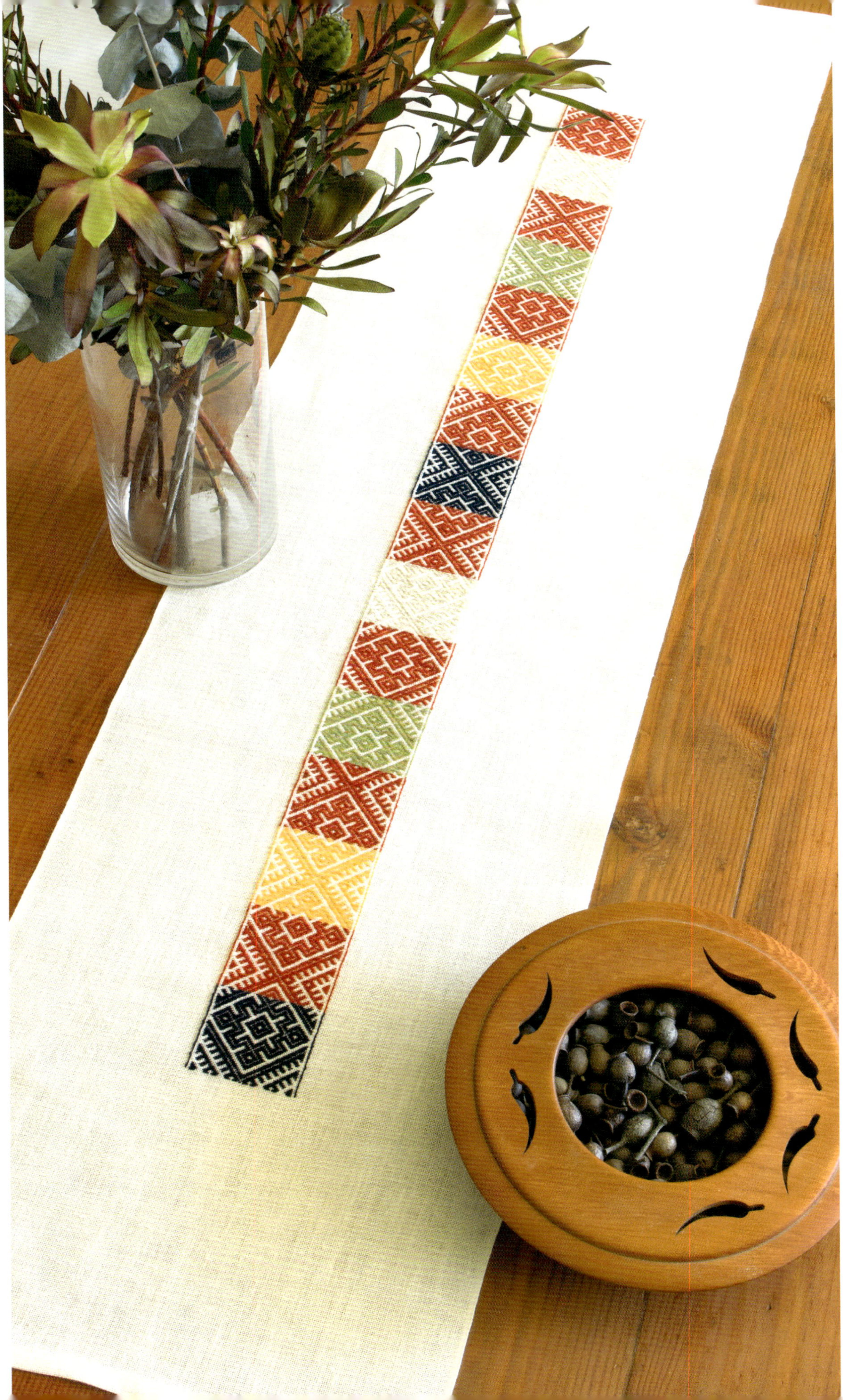

table runner

This table runner has a simple repeating band down the centre. The coloured stripes are typical of the smøyg used on likkross (ceremonial cloths) from Telemark.

size 30 x 116 cm / 12 x 45½ in
design thread dimensions 61(w) x 912 (h) threads
materials and equipment

- Rustic Wool Moire threads, 1 reel each: 120 (stone), 211 (yellow), 280 (red), 403 (green), 591 (blue)
  OR
  Gumnut Yarns Daisies, 1 skein each: 349 (blue), 645 (green), 728 (yellow), 963 (stone)
  2 skeins: 859 (red)
- 1.2 m (47 in) Vaupel and Heilenbeck linen banding, 900/300, 30cm wide, 28 count
- machine-sewing thread to match linen
- No 22 tapestry needle

Note on threads: Rustic Wool Moire threads (see below) have flecks of other colours in them and are worth seeking out. However, if they are not available, substitute two strands of Gumnut Yarns Daisies, and use a laying tool.

preparation

1 Fold 1cm (⅜ in) of the fabric in at each end. Enclosing the raw edge, fold in another 1cm (⅜ in). Sew close to the first fold, across each end. Neatly finish the thread ends.
❶ *The hems will sit on the back.*
2 Fold the fabric in half both ways to find the centre. From the centre, including the centre thread, count 31 threads out toward one of the long sides of the fabric. Run a line of tacking down the entire length of the runner.
3 From the centre, including the centre thread, count 31 threads out toward the opposite side of the fabric. Run a line of tacking down the entire length of the runner.

embroidery

❶ *Follow the chart for stitch and colour placement.*
❶ *The centre is marked on the chart with arrows.*
1 The starting point is where the centre fold passes through one of the tacked lines.
2 Work the blue block adjacent to the centre marker.
❶ *The row ends are worked as front border turns.*
3 Continue along the runner towards the end, changing colours as required.
4 From the centre, work to the other end, changing colours as required.

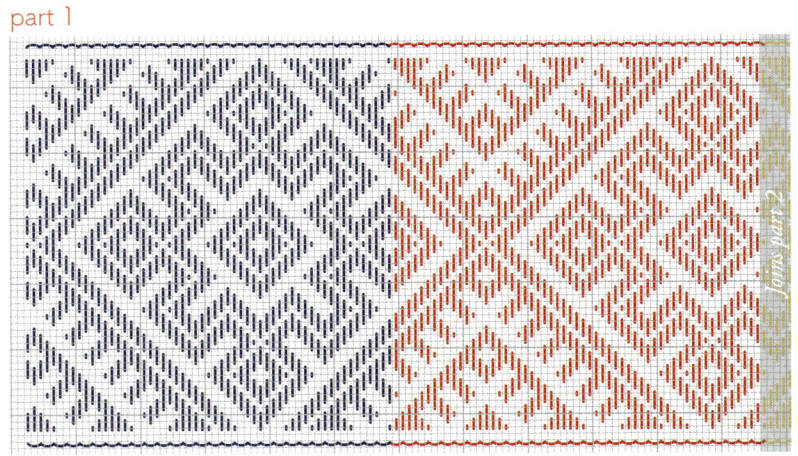

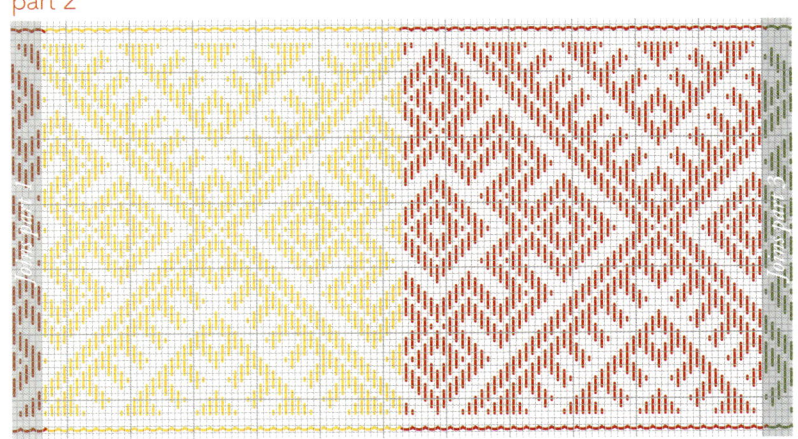

part 1

part 2

part 3

part 4

part 5

part 6

espresso pendant

This pendant is worked on 50 count linen, so it isn't for the faint-hearted. The espresso coloured silk thread was chosen as many of the old examples using black silk have faded unevenly to brown. This overdyed thread simulates that effect.

size 2.5 x 5 cm / 1 x 2 in
design thread dimensions 45 (w) x 104 (h) threads
materials and equipment
- 15 x 15 cm (6 x 6 in) 50 count linen, white
- No 26 tapestry needle
- 1 skein Classic Colorworks Belle Soie Silk, Espresso
- 12.5 cm (5 in) hoop
- rectangular pendant tray, fits 2.5 x 5 cm (1 x 2 in)
- 50 cm (20 in) chain
- 2.4 x 4.9 cm ($^{15}/_{16}$ x 1 $^{15}/_{16}$ in) acid-free cardboard, white
- machine-sewing thread, white
- very strong double-sided adhesive tape, acid-free

embroidery

❶ *Follow the chart for stitch placement.*
1 From the top left corner of the linen, measure across 5 cm (2 in). From there, measure down 6.5 cm (2$^{9}/_{16}$ in). This is the point to start stitching the top left corner.
2 Mount the fabric in a hoop so that it is drum tight.
3 Work the design in running stitch.

construction

1 Trim the fabric around the design to 1.5 cm (⅝ in) away from the edge of the stitching.
2 With the embroidery right side out, and centred on the cardboard, lace the embroidery over the cardboard.
3 Cut double-sided adhesive to fit the pendant tray. Peel off the tape covering the adhesive.
4 Press the embroidery into the tray so that a strong bond is formed.

band sampler

Traditionally, samplers were a record of motifs and stitches, for use on other articles. This bell-pull sampler is a project in its own right, but also used as a menu of designs from which to choose for other projects. The bands come from many different garments, across a number of regions.

size approximately 11.5 x 123 cm / 4½ x 48½ in
design thread dimensions   138 (w) x 1604 (h) threads
materials and equipment

- 25 x 140 cm (10 x 55 in) 34 count linen, white
- Fine d'Aubusson wool, 1 skein each: 125, 126, 514, 542, 543, 1012, 1727, 1770, 1811, 1836, 2118, 2132, 2154, 2525, 2542, 2636, 2770, 2808, 2952, 3020, 3046, 3084, 3220, 3221, 3318, 3484, 3724, 3825, 4102, 4147, 4216, 4612, 4633, 5382
  2 skeins each: 916, 2924, 4106
- Mora wool, 10 m each: 2010, 2013, 2024, 2044, 2061, 2062
- DMC pearl cotton 8, 1 ball 311
- Au Ver à Soie, Soie d'Alger, 1 skein each: 4106, 4246
- Au Ver à Soie, Soie Ovale, 2 reels noir
- Au Ver à Soie, Soie Perlée, 1 reel each: 102, 740
- No 24 tapestry needle
- No 24 chenille needle
- laying tool or large chenille needle, e.g. No 20
- 12 cm (4¾ in) bell-pull hangers
- machine-sewing thread to match dyed linen
- 17.5 cm (7 in) embroidery hoop
- tea bag

preparation

1 Make weak to medium tea using the tea bag and boiling water. Dip the fabric. Dry and assess the colour. To darken it, dip it more times until happy with the colour.

❶ *The colour is darker when it is wet. Dye it gradually to build up the colour, rather than using a strong tea solution.*

2 Rinse the fabric to ensure there is no excess dye left.
3 Measure 7 cm (3 in) from one of the long sides of the fabric. Run a line of tacking down the length of the fabric.
4 Count 138 threads across the fabric width and run another line of tacking down the length of the fabric.
5 Measure 10 cm (4 in) from the top end. Starting just outside of the tacked guides, tack across the width, to just outside the other guide.
6 Count down 79 threads and tack another line across, thus completing the area for band 1.
7 Band 2: Count down 8 threads and tack a line across. Count down 51 threads and tack another line.

8 Band 3: Count down 8 threads and tack a line across. Count down 97 threads and tack another line.
9 Band 4: Count down 8 threads and tack a line across. Count down 45 threads and tack another line.
10 Band 5: Count down 8 threads and tack a line across. Count down 131 threads and tack another line.
11 Band 6: Count down 8 threads and tack a line across. Count down 27 threads and tack another line.
12 Band 7: Count down 8 threads and tack a line across. Count down 38 threads and tack another line.
13 Band 8: Count down 8 threads and tack a line across. Count down 109 threads and tack another line.
14 Band 9: Count down 8 threads and tack a line across. Count down 67 threads and tack another line.
15 Band 10: Count down 8 threads and tack a line across. Count down 23 threads and tack another line.
16 Band 11: Count down 8 threads and tack a line across. Count down 129 threads and tack another line.
17 Band 12: Count down 8 threads and tack a line across. Count down 50 threads and tack another line.
18 Band 13: Count down 8 threads and tack a line across. Count down 21 threads and tack another line.
19 Band 14: Count down 8 threads and tack a line across. Count down 107 threads and tack another line.
20 Band 15: Count down 8 threads and tack a line across. Count down 49 threads and tack another line.
21 Band 16: Count down 8 threads and tack a line across. Count down 39 threads and tack another line.
22 Band 17: Count down 8 threads and tack a line across. Count down 107 threads and tack another line.
23 Band 18: Count down 8 threads and tack a line across. Count down 35 threads and tack another line.
24 Band 19: Count down 8 threads and tack a line across. Count down 35 threads and tack another line.
25 Band 20: Count down 8 threads and tack a line across. Count down 107 threads and tack another line.
26 Band 21: Count down 8 threads and tack a line across. Count down 49 threads and tack another line.
27 Band 22: Count down 8 threads and tack a line across. Count down 41 threads and tack another line.

tacking diagram

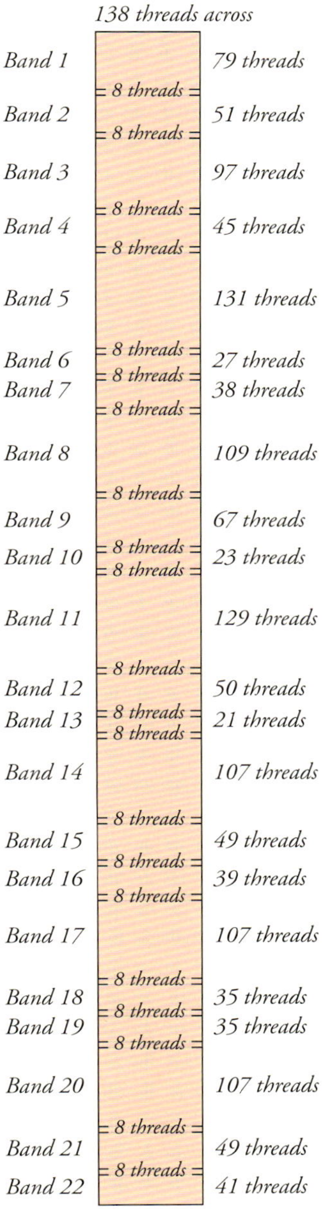

138 threads across

Band 1	79 threads
8 threads	
Band 2	51 threads
8 threads	
Band 3	97 threads
8 threads	
Band 4	45 threads
8 threads	
Band 5	131 threads
8 threads	
Band 6	27 threads
8 threads	
Band 7	38 threads
8 threads	
Band 8	109 threads
8 threads	
Band 9	67 threads
8 threads	
Band 10	23 threads
8 threads	
Band 11	129 threads
8 threads	
Band 12	50 threads
8 threads	
Band 13	21 threads
8 threads	
Band 14	107 threads
8 threads	
Band 15	49 threads
8 threads	
Band 16	39 threads
8 threads	
Band 17	107 threads
8 threads	
Band 18	35 threads
8 threads	
Band 19	35 threads
8 threads	
Band 20	107 threads
8 threads	
Band 21	49 threads
8 threads	
Band 22	41 threads

embroidery

❶ *All embroidery uses the tapestry needle unless otherwise directed. Running stitch the entire project except where indicated. Follow the chart for stitch and colour placement.*

Mount the fabric in a hoop, with the band you're working on centred. Move the hoop as required.

band 1

This design comes from a belt from Hordaland. Based on NF 2000-1699. Height: 79 threads.

Black: Fine d'Aubusson 4106
Cream: Fine d'Aubusson 3020
Green: Fine d'Aubusson 3724
Red: Fine d'Aubusson 916

Work the red above the first black motif's position. At its end, continue to the band's lower edge, working the full length until you reach the next black motif, then continue above it. Repeat as required. Work the red sections below the black motifs. Work the black motifs. Work the cream and green with the chenille needle.

band 2

This design comes from a bridegroom's handkerchief from Telemark. Based on NF 1921-0661. Height: 51 threads.
Blue: Mora 2062
Grey: Fine d'Aubusson 3221
Green: Fine d'Aubusson 3318
Red: Fine d'Aubusson 916
Straw: Fine d'Aubusson 2542
Work each section in turn.

band 3

This design comes from a shirt collar from Telemark. Based on TGM-SM.3418. Height: 97 threads.
Chocolate: Fine d'Aubusson 1770
Work the band using running stitch.

band 4

This design comes from a shirt collar from Buskerud. Based on NF 1992-2285AC. Height: 45 threads.
Black: Fine d'Aubusson 4106
Blue: Fine d'Aubusson 125
Green: Fine d'Aubusson 1836
Red: Fine d'Aubusson 916
Yellow: Fine d'Aubusson 542
Work the black left end, then the red middle, then the black right end. Work all other colours with a chenille needle.

band 5

This design comes from a shirt collar from Telemark. Based on SM1055-1545. Height: 131 threads.
Brown: Fine d'Aubusson 2808
Green: Fine d'Aubusson 2118
Pink: Fine d'Aubusson 4147
Russet: Fine d'Aubusson 2636
Tan: Fine d'Aubusson 3825
Work the green. Change to the chenille needle. Stitch the tan diagonal lines. Work the kinnekrosses and remaining diagonals in russet. Work the Ss in pink. Work the large and small diamonds and small Vs in brown.

38

band 6

This design comes from the strap on a baby cap from Setesdal. Based on NF.1949-0525. Height: 27 threads.

Blue: DMC No 8 pearl cotton, 311
Grey: Fine d'Aubusson 1811
Red: Fine d'Aubusson 2924
Work each section in turn.

band 7

This design comes from a border on a baby cap. Based on FYB.00097. Height: 38 threads.

Green: Fine d'Aubusson 514
Red: Fine d'Aubusson 916
Work the green at the top, then at the bottom. Work the red between.

band 8

This design comes from the collar of a shirt. Based on TGM-SM.2461. Height: 109 threads.

Black: Soie Ovale, noir
Work the band using a laying tool.

band 9

This design comes from a likkross (ceremonial cloth), from Telemark. Based on NF.2001-0067A. Height: 67 threads.

Blue: Fine d'Aubusson 1727
Green: Fine d'Aubusson 1826
Red: Fine d'Aubusson 2924
Work each section in turn.

band 10

This design comes from a border on a bridegroom's handkerchief from Telemark. Based on NF.1992-2384. Height: 23 threads.

Blue: Mora 2061
Green: Fine d'Aubusson 2952
Red: Fine d'Aubusson 2924
Work each section in turn using front border turns.

band 11

This design comes from the collar of a shirt from Telemark. Based on TGM-SM.0794. Height: 129 threads.

Apricot: Fine d'Aubusson 1012
Beige: Fine d'Aubusson 3084
Beige silk: Soie Perlée 740
Black: Fine d'Aubusson 4106

Brown: Fine d'Aubusson 4216
Cream: Fine d'Aubusson 4102
Cream silk: Soie Perlée 102
Green: Fine d'Aubusson 2118
Red: Mora 2024
Yellow: Mora 2044

Work the beige diagonals. From the left edge, work the yellow; upper part first, then the remaining lower part. Work the black diamond; upper part first, then lower part. Change to the chenille needle. Stitch the red meandering line, and the Ss in alternating cream and beige silk. Use the cream silk for the small diamonds in the corners of the yellow diagonals. Work the small diamonds in the beige diagonals in satin stitch with cream wool. Work the corners and centre diamond in satin stitch, following the chart for stitch placement, direction and colour. The centre cross is cream wool.

band 12

From a collar and cuffs from Hallingdal. Unusually, the running stitch goes across the band rather than down it. Based on NF.1992-2537. Height: 50 threads.
Dark green: Fine d'Aubusson 1836
Mid green: Fine d'Aubusson 2118
Red: Fine d'Aubusson 2924
Stitch each section in turn.

band 13

This design comes from the sleeve of a shirt from Telemark. On the sleeve it is stitched in very fluffy wool. Based on NF.2000-0612. Height: 21 threads.
Blue: Fine d'Aubusson 126
Caramel: Fine d'Aubusson 2770
Plum: Fine d'Aubusson 3046
Yellow: Fine d'Aubusson 543
Work each section in turn using front border turns.

band 14

This design comes from a shirt collar from Telemark. Based on TGM-SM.0868. Height: 107 threads.
Black: Fine d'Aubusson 4106
Work the band.

Band 4

Band 6 and 7

Band 15 and 16

Band 17

Band 22

41

band 15

From a belt from Hordaland. Based on BUM.2047. Height: 49 threads.

Green: Fine d'Aubusson 2132
Red: Fine d'Aubusson 916
Stitch each section in turn.

band 16

From a likkross (ceremonial cloth) from Telemark. Based on NF.2001-0067A. Height: 39 threads.

Mid blue: Fine d'Aubusson 2154
Green: Mora 2013
Light blue: Fine d'Aubusson 5382
Red: Fine d'Aubusson 2924
Work each section in turn using front border turns.

band 17

This design comes from a collar from Telemark. Based on TGM-SM.2542. Height: 107 threads.

Caramel: Fine d'Aubusson 2770
Mauve: Fine d'Aubusson 4633
Pale brown: Fine d'Aubusson 3484
Straw: Fine d'Aubusson 2542
There is no easy way to divide this up! Just work it in small sections. Work the caramel and pale brown. Work the straw and mauve diamonds in satin stitch using the chenille needle.

band 18

This design comes from the sleeves of a shirt from Telemark. Based on NF.1992-1832. Height: 35 threads.

Green: Fine d'Aubusson 2952
Grey: Fine d'Aubusson 3220
Red: Fine d'Aubusson 916
Yellow: Fine d'Aubusson 2525
Work each section in turn using front border turns.

band 19

This design comes from the front yoke of a shirt from Hordaland. Based on HFU.3119. Height: 35 threads.

Black: 2 strands Soie d'Alger, 4106.
Work the band using a laying tool.

band 20

This design comes from a shirt collar from Telemark. Based on TGM-BM.1915:093. Height: 107 threads.
Blue: Fine d'Aubusson 5382
Brown: Fine d'Aubusson 2636
Dark green: Fine d'Aubusson 2952
Orange: Fine d'Aubusson 4612
Pale green: Fine d'Aubusson 2132
Work the pale green, dark green and centre section of orange. Change to the chenille needle. Work the diamonds in satin stitch and the remaining stitching in running stitch.

band 21

This design comes from a border on a baby wrap from Setesdal. Based on NF.1897-0564. Height: 49 threads.
Green: Mora 2010
Red: Mora 2024
Work each section in turn.

band 22

This design comes from a shirt collar from Hordaland. Based on NF.1955-0378. Height: 41 threads.
Brown: 2 strands Soie d'Alger, 4246.
Work the band using a laying tool.

construction

1 With right sides facing, bring the long edges together. Using a 1cm (⅜ in) seam allowance, sew the length of the fabric, leaving a 10 cm (4 in) gap in the centre of the seam. Press the seam allowance open.

2 Centre the embroidery on one side, with the seam in the middle of the back. Sew across the width at each end 5 cm (2 in) from the end of the embroidery. Trim the seam allowance to 1cm (⅜ in).

3 Turn the bellpull the right way out through the gap in the seam. Neatly handstitch the gap closed.

4 Fold 2cm (⅞ in) to the back at each end. Sew 1.5cm (⅝ in) from the fold to make rod pockets.

5 Remove all tacking.

6 Press. Insert the hangers.

bookmarks

These bookmarks are an excellent place to start your smøyg exploration. The beginner one has a single layer of stitching with a self-striping overdyed thread, and the intermediate one has the addition of stitched stripes.

size 30 x 6 cm / 12 x 2⅜ in

design thread dimensions 170 (w) x 51 (h) threads

materials and equipment

- 30 cm (12 in) Vaupel and Heilenbeck linen banding, 900/060, 6 cm (2⅜ in) wide, 28 count, per bookmark
- No 22 tapestry needle
- stranded embroidery floss, DMC712

For the self-striping beginner bookmark:

- 10 m skein Misti Alpaca Handpaint Laceweight 53

❶ *This is a discontinued knitting yarn, however small skeins for embroidery are available from Vetty Creations until stocks last. Alternatively, you can use any thin overdyed 2 ply yarn, where the colours don't change too quickly.*

For the stitched stripes intermediate bookmark:

- Gumnut Yarns Daisies, 1 skein each: 555 (green), 726 (yellow), 329 (blue), 857 (red)
- laying tool or large chenille needle, e.g. No 20

embroidery

❶ *Follow the chart for stitch and colour placement.*

1 Measure 7 cm (2¾ in) from one end of the linen banding. From one side, count nine threads across. This is the starting point for stitching, and the corner of the design.

❶ *Because of the number of threads across the width, there will be nine threads on one side and ten on the other.*

2 Beginner Stitch the whole design in the one colour. Use backstitch turns at both ends of the rows as this provides a neater look on the back, which will be seen.

2 Intermediate Using two strands of the Daisies yarn and the laying tool to lay the stitches correctly, running stitch each section in turn. Use backstitch turns at both ends of the rows as this provides a neater look on the back, which will be seen.

3 Count eight threads out from one end of the embroidery. Using one strand of the stranded floss, work a line of satin stitch from edge to edge, with each stitch spanning three threads.

4 Repeat the satin stitch bar at the other end.

5 Undo the weaving at each end up to the satin stitched bars, to create a fringe. Trim the unwoven thread 7 cm (2¾ in) from the fringe. Thread it into a needle and run it under the back of the satin stitch for 2–3 cm (¾–1¼ in). Trim any excess. ❦

The back, showing the backstitch turns at the row ends.

45

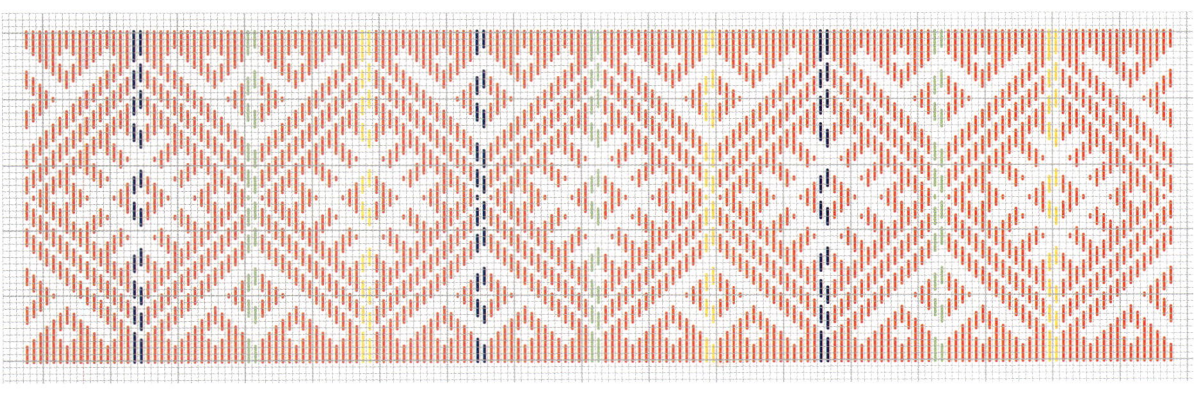

hanging ornament

This Christmas tree ornament was designed to evoke the warmth of a woolly Norwegian knitted sweater on a snowy day.

size 7 x 7 cm / 2¾ x 2¾ in
design thread dimensions 101 (w) x 63 (h) threads
materials and equipment

- 15 x 15 cm (6 x 6 in) 40 count linen, white
- Devere Yarns No 36 silk, Poppy/109
- Au Ver à Soie, Soie Perlée, 102, 323
- No 24 tapestry needle
- No 24 chenille needle
- No 9 embroidery needle
- 12.5 cm (5 in) hoop
- 23 cm (9 in) Lady Dot Creates cotton chenille, Snow
- narrow satin ribbon, white, 16 cm (6¼ in) long
- 2, 6 cm (2⅜ in) diameter circles of wadding
- 2, 6 cm (2⅜ in) diameter circles of heavy weight acid-free card
- 8 cm (3⅛ in) diameter circle of backing fabric
- machine-sewing thread, white

❶ *Templates for the circles are provided on the pattern sheet inside the back cover of the book.*

embroidery

❶ *All embroidery uses the tapestry needle unless otherwise directed. Follow the chart for stitch and colour placement.*

1 From the top left corner of the linen, measure across 4 cm (1½ in). From this point, measure down 5.5 cm (2¼ in). This is the starting point for the top left corner.
2 Mount the fabric in a hoop so that it is drum tight.
3 Work the red stitching in running stitch using the Devere Yarns silk.
4 Work the gold stitching in satin stitch, using the Soie Perlée 323 and the chenille needle.
5 Work the white stitching in running stitch, using the Soie Perlée 102 and the chenille needle.

construction

1 With the embroidery carefully centred, cut an 8 cm (3⅛ in) circle from the linen.
2 With a doubled length of machine-sewing thread, running stitch around the edge of the fabric circle, 5 mm (³⁄₁₆ in) from the cut edge, leaving 15 cm (6 in) of thread hanging at each end of the stitching.
3 Lay a circle of wadding over one cardboard circle. With cardboard on top, and wadding below, centre them on the back of the embroidered circle.
4 Pull up the gathering threads and tie the ends securely. Trim the gathering threads.
5 Repeat with the backing fabric and wadding for the back.
6 Thread a length of machine-sewing thread into the needle. Fold the ribbon in half and attach it, with a seam allowance of about 8 mm (⁵⁄₁₆ in), to the back of the front panel, at the top. Continuing with the same thread, ladder stitch the front and back of the ornament together.
7 Starting just beside the ribbon, take 6–8 mm (¼–⁵⁄₁₆ in) long stitches through the rim of the ornament and couch the chenille edging to the ornament.
8 Make a small overlap at the end, and then trim any extra chenille.

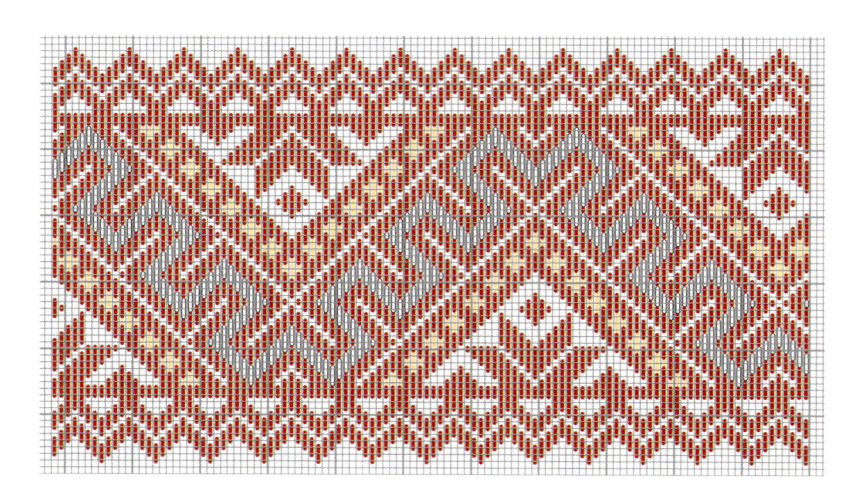

table centre

This table centre features the type of smøyg found on likkross (ceremonial cloths) from Notodden in Aust-Telemark. This smøyg was usually worked in a browny black silk. It is hard to know whether that was the original colour, or whether black silk faded to brown.

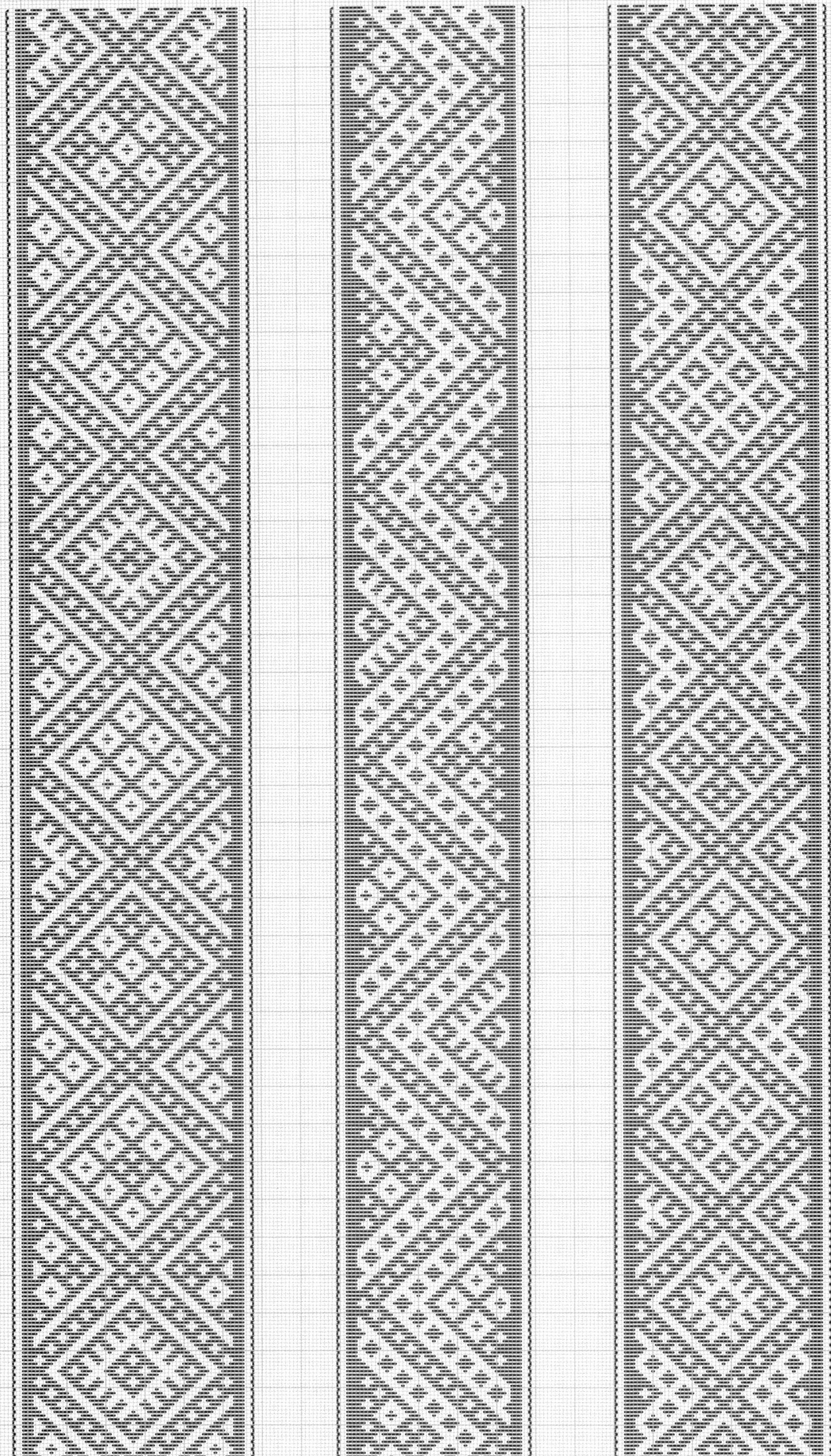

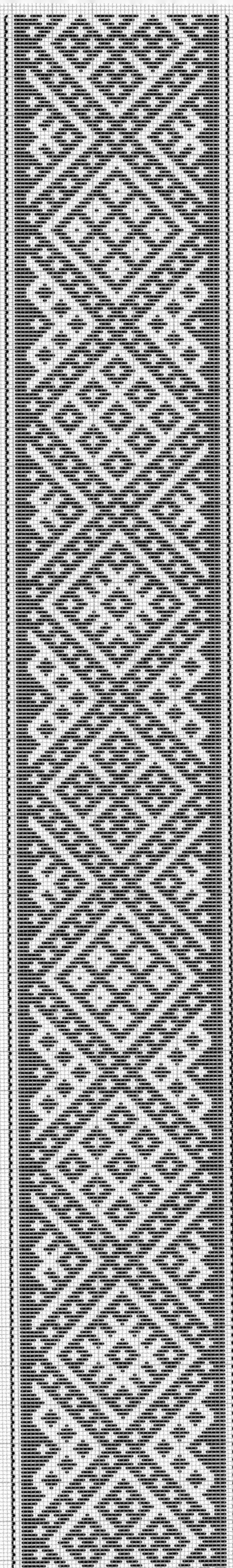
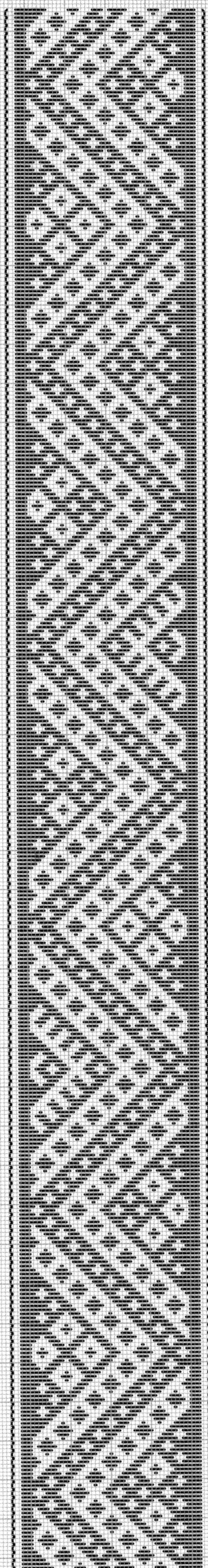
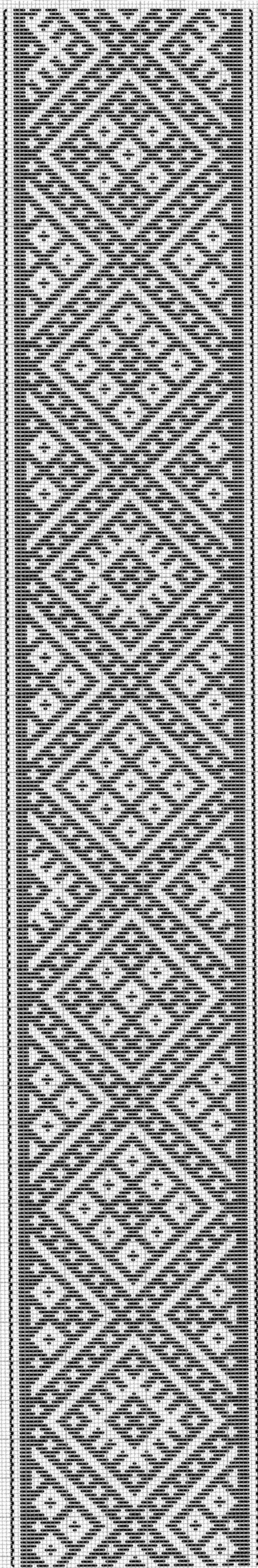

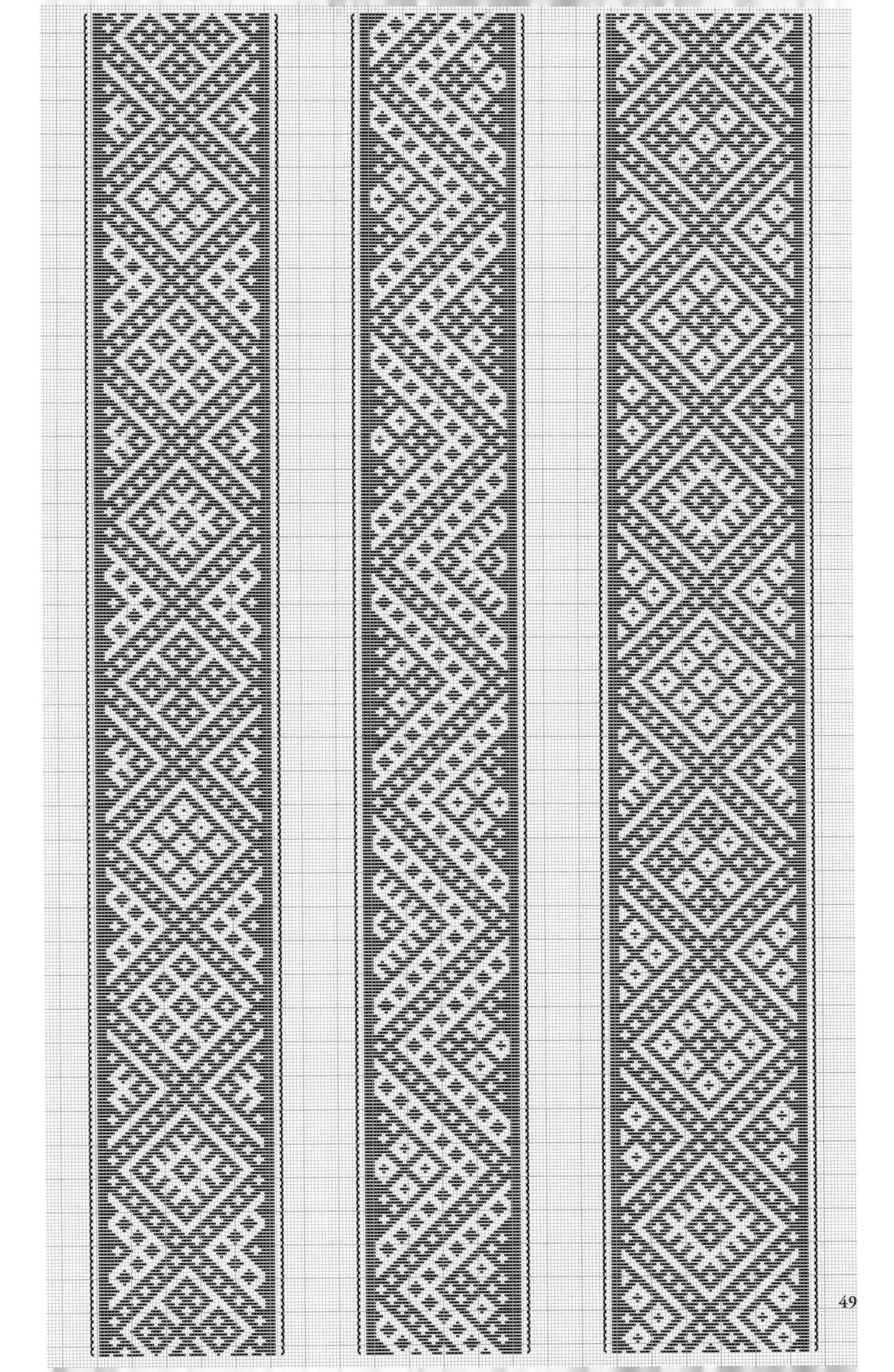

size 52 x 34.5 cm / 20 ½ x 13 ½ in
design thread dimensions 398(w) x 618 (h) threads
materials and equipment
- 60 x 40 cm (23 ½ x 15 ¾ in) 40 count linen, cream
- 3 reels of Devere Yarns No 36 silk, Harness/134
- No 24 tapestry needle
- 20 cm (8 in) hoop
- machine-sewing thread to match fabric and a pale colour

preparation

1 Fold the fabric in half both ways to find the centre.
2 With a long length of the pale coloured machine-sewing thread, insert the needle at the centre. Leaving a long tail at the centre, and tacking towards one of the short ends, take the needle under five threads then over five threads. Continue tacking under and over groups of five threads to the edge of the fabric.
3 Thread the long tail into the needle. Heading to the opposite end, take the needle over five threads, then under five threads. Continue tacking over and under groups of five threads to the edge of the fabric.
4 From the centre, count 20 groups (100 threads) along the tacked line towards one end.
5 At the end of the 20th group, insert a needle threaded with a long length of the pale thread. Leaving a long tail at the centre, and tacking towards one of the long sides, take the needle under five threads then over five threads. Continue tacking under and over groups of five threads to the edge of the fabric.
6 Thread the long tail into the needle. Heading to the opposite side, take the needle over five threads, then under five threads. Continue tacking over and under groups of five threads to the edge of the fabric.
7 Count another 11 groups (55 threads) further along the first tacked line.
8 At the end of the 11th group, insert a needle threaded with a long length of the pale thread. Leaving a long tail at the centre, and tacking towards one of the long sides, take the needle under five threads then over five threads. Continue tacking under and over groups of five threads to the edge of the fabric.
9 Thread the long tail into the needle. Heading to the opposite side, take the needle over five threads, then under five threads. Continue tacking over and under groups of five threads to the edge of the fabric.
10 Using the counted tacking to assist, count 22 threads further along the first tacked guide and work another line of tacking across the fabric.
11 Count 49 threads further and work another line.
12 Count 22 threads further and work another line.
13 Count 61 threads further and work another line.
14 Repeat this sequence of tacking at the other end.
15 From the centre guide, count 199 threads out along the first perpendicular tacked guide. Work a line of tacking that is parallel to the long side of the fabric at this point.
16 Repeat on the other side.

embroidery

❶ *Follow the chart for stitch placement.*
1 Mount the fabric in a hoop so that it is drum tight. Move the hoop as required as you stitch.
2 Work the pattern darning on the left end of the cloth using the chart on page 48, working front border turns at the ends of the rows.
3 Work the pattern darning on the right end of the cloth using the chart on page 49, working front border turns at the ends of the rows.

hemming

1 Measure 9 cm (3 ⁹⁄₁₆ in) from one of the end bands of stitching. Trim the end of the cloth at this point. Repeat at the other end of the cloth.
2 Measure 7cm (2 ¾ in) from the ends of the embroidered bands. Trim the sides of the cloth at these points.
3 Work 1cm (⅜ in) hems with mitred corners.
4 Machine stitch the hems in place, 2 mm (¹⁄₁₆ in) away from the inside edge of the hem.
5 Remove the tacking.

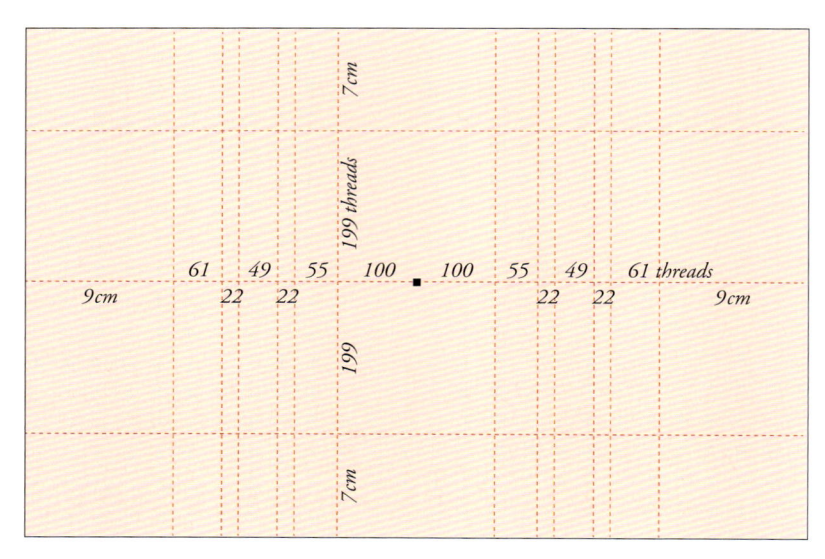

poppy pendant

This pendant was designed to look as if someone has decided to feature a special part of an old piece of pattern darning. Of course, it isn't old at all, but custom created. The poppy red could be replaced with your colour of choice.

size 3.8 x 3.8 cm / 1 ½ x 1 ½ in
design thread dimensions
66 (w) x 68 (h) threads
materials and equipment
- 15 x 15 cm (6 x 6 in) 40 count linen, white
- No 24 tapestry needle
- 1 reel of Devere Yarns No 36 silk, Poppy/109
- 12.5 cm (5 in) hoop
- circular pendant tray, fits 3.8 cm (1 ½ in) diameter
- 50 cm (20 in) chain
- 3.7 cm (1 7/16 in) circle of acid-free cardboard, white

A circle template is provided on the pattern sheet.

- machine-sewing thread, white
- very strong double-sided adhesive tape, acid-free

embroidery

Follow the chart for stitch placement.

1 From the top left corner of the linen, measure across 5.5 cm (2 3/16 in). From this point, measure down 8 cm (3 1/8 in). This is the starting point for the lower end of the left-most row.
2 Mount the fabric in a hoop so that it is drum tight.
3 Work the design in running stitch.

construction

1 Cut around the design 1 cm (3/8 in) away from the edge of the stitching.
2 With a doubled length of machine-sewing thread, running stitch around the edge of the fabric circle, 5 mm (3/16 in) from the cut edge, leaving 15 cm (6 in) of thread hanging at each end of the stitching.
3 Lay the embroidery face down.
4 Centre the cardboard circle over the embroidery.
5 Gather up the running stitch thread around the cardboard circle. Tightly tie it off. Trim the excess thread.
6 Cut pieces of shaped double-sided adhesive to fit in the pendant tray. Peel off the tape covering the adhesive.
7 Carefully position the embroidery over the pendant tray, making sure the horizontal line near the top of the embroidery will hang horizontally in the pendant. Press the embroidery into the tray so that a strong bond is formed.

cushion

This cushion features the type of smøyg found on baby wraps from Setesdal in Aust-Agder. The stitching is usually predominantly red, with spot motifs in other colours, and multiple borders in striping colours.

cushion size 38 x 25 cm / 15 x 10 in
design thread dimensions 261 (w) x 340 (h) threads

materials and equipment
- 35 x 40 cm (14 x 16 in) 34 count linen, white
- Mora wool, 30 m 2010, 40 m 2062, 70 m 2024
- No 24 tapestry needle
- 60 cm (24 in) navy blue satin piping
- 30 cm (12 in) red fabric
- 25 cm (10 in) invisible zip, red
- machine-sewing thread, red, white and a pale colour
- 28 x 79 cm (11 x 31 in) polycotton fabric, white
- 20 cm (8 in) embroidery hoop
- polyester fibre fill

preparation

1 With the linen fabric in landscape orientation, measure 7.5 cm (3 in) from one corner, along the top. From this point, tack a line down the fabric with the pale-coloured machine-sewing thread.
2 From the tacked guide, count 340 threads across the fabric, and run another tacked line down the fabric.
❶ *These lines form the embroidery's side edges when looking at the embroidered panel in a landscape orientation.*
3 Measure 8.5 cm (3¼ in) from the corner, down the side of the fabric. From this point, run another tacked line across the fabric.
4 From the tacked guide, count 261 threads down the fabric, and run another tacked line across the fabric.
❶ *These lines form the top and bottom edges of the embroidery.*
5 From the top tacked guide, count down 37 threads and run another line across between the side guides.
❶ *This guide forms the bottom of the boat motif border.*

embroidery

❶ *Follow the chart for stitch and colour placement.*
1 Mount the fabric in a hoop so that it is drum tight. Move the hoop as required as you work.
2 Work the border along the top edge (with the boat motifs) in stripes.
3 Work the upper border of meandering lines, in stripes.
❶ *The thin line of stripes is worked as part of this border.*
4 Work the red in the centre section of the embroidery, dividing it in sections as shown in the diagram below.
5 Work the blue motifs in the centre section.
6 Work the green motifs in the centre section.
7 Work the lower border in stripes.
❶ *The thin line of stripes is worked as part of this border.*

cushion construction

❶ *Use a 1.5 cm (⅝ in) seam allowance throughout.*
1 From the red fabric, cut the following pieces: 8.5 x 28 cm (3½ x 11 in), 16 x 28 cm (6¼ x 11 in), and 41 x 28 cm (16 x 11 in).
2 Trim the sides of the embroidered panel to 1.8 cm (¾ in) on the border sides of the embroidery. Trim the ends to 1.5 cm (⅝ in) from the ends of the embroidery.
3 Lay the piping down the boat side of the embroidery, so that the stitching lines for the piping and cushion align.
4 Baste it in place.
5 Repeat for the other side.
6 With right sides together, sew the 8.5 cm (3½ in) wide piece of red fabric to the boat side of the design.
7 With right sides together, sew the 16 cm (6¼ in) wide piece of red fabric to the opposite side of the design.
8 Fold the seam allowances at the back towards the embroidered panel.
9 Insert the zip at the end of the cushion with the 16 cm (6¼ in) piece of red fabric.
10 With right sides together, sew the remaining three sides of the cushion.
11 Turn the cushion the right way out through the zip.

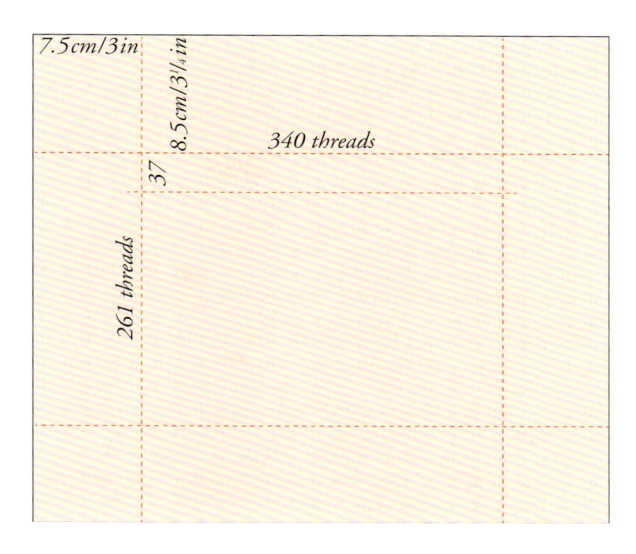

cushion insert

1 Fold the polycotton fabric in half, matching the raw edges. Sew around the three sides with raw edges, leaving a 10 cm (4 in) gap at the end of the last side.
2 Turn the cushion insert right side out.
3 Stuff with polyester fibre fill.
4 Hand stitch the gap closed.
5 Insert the cushion insert into the cushion cover and close the zip. ✿

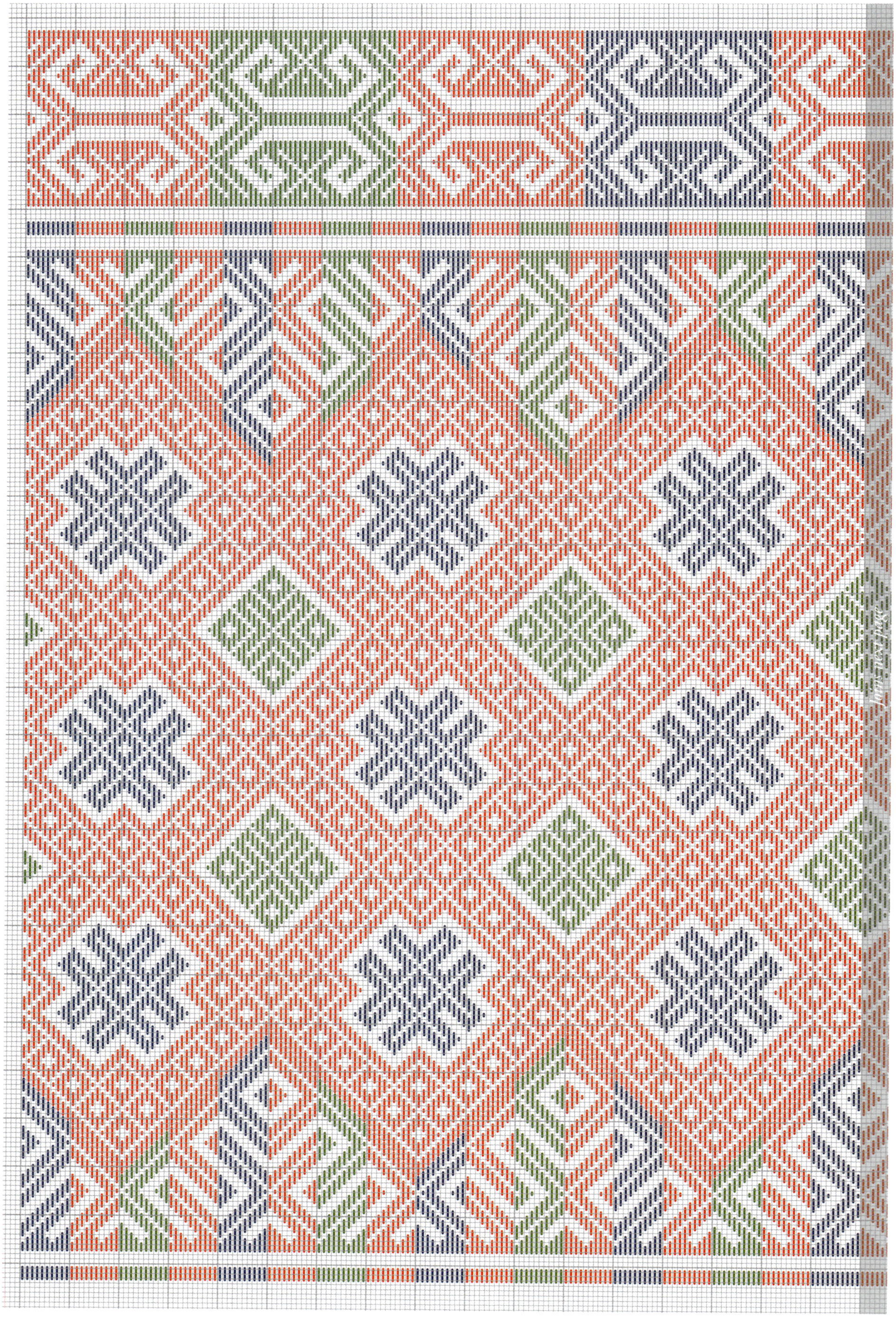

55

shirt

This is a shirt with a modern cut that features smøyg on the collar. It does not try to copy the style of traditional Norwegian folk dress shirts.

design thread dimensions
Size A: 672, B: 704, C: 736, D: 768 (w) x 103 (h) threads

materials and equipment
- 60 x 40 cm (23 ½ x 15 ¾ in) 40 count linen, antique white
- linen dress fabric, medium weight, to match colour
- ❕ *See the pattern sheet for quantity.*
- Fine d'Aubusson wool, 1 skein each: 946, 2926, 3825
- Fine d'Aubusson wool, 3 skeins: 1847
- Mora wool, 60m 2013
- No 24 tapestry needle
- No 24 chenille needle
- 20 cm (8 in) hoop
- 8 buttons, 12 mm (½ in) diameter
- 3 large sheets of paper, at least 67 x 38 cm (27 x 15 in)
- machine-sewing thread to match fabric

❕ *The shirt pattern is found on the pattern sheet inside the back cover of the book.*

preparation
1 Wash all the fabric to pre-shrink it.
2 Choose a garment size from the pattern sheet chart.
3 Trace the pattern pieces and all markings onto the large pieces of paper. Cut them out.
4 Lay out the pattern pieces on the fabric. Pin them in place and cut them out.
5 Transfer the tailor's markings to the fabric.
6 Fold the embroidery linen in half both ways. From where the folds intersect, count down twelve threads. This will be the centre top of the pattern darning. Run a line of tacking along the length of the fabric from this point. Count down another 103 threads. Run another line across the fabric from this point. Work a line of tacking down the fold that intersects these two lines.

embroidery
❕ *All embroidery uses the tapestry needle unless otherwise directed. Follow the chart for stitch and colour placement.*
❕ *Note that the charts start and finish in different places, and have different centres, depending on the collar/shirt size.*

1 Work the blue green diamonds, dividing them into a top half and bottom half, so that the thread doesn't carry across the gaps in the middle.
2 Work the very dark green triangles at the sides, and the double diamonds in the centres.
3 Work the orange centres.
4 Work the maroon diamonds just outside the very dark green diamonds.
❕ *Use the chenille needle for the remainder of the embroidery.*
5 Work the red infills around the orange centres, and in the side triangles. Also work the red Ss.
6 Work the very dark green bars in the orange centres.
7 Work the blue green bars in the side triangles.
8 Work the orange diamonds in the side triangles.
9 Count up eight threads from the embroidery and withdraw the next eight threads across the length of the fabric.
10 Using the blue green wool, work the woven bars of the tooth edging, grouping threads in threes (six threads per bar), aligning the row ends with the embroidery ends.
❕ *For Size A and D, the quantity of threads works perfectly with groups of six threads. For Size B, there are two extra threads, so the first and last group of three threads will need to be four threads. For Size C, there are four extra threads, so the first two and last two groups of three will need to be four threads.*
12 Trim the ends of the embroidered panel to 1cm (⅜ in), and continue cutting right across the fabric.
13 Fold the fabric in half along the woven bars. Match the raw ends, and with the back of the embroidery up, carefully sew along each end of the embroidery, right at the edge of the stitching.
14 Neatly trim the unwoven threads where the drawn thread and seam allowance areas intersect. Turn the collar right side out, again folding the bars in half.
15 Work the stitches between the bars in the red wool.
16 Work the backstitch part of the kvalesaum using the blue green wool.
❕ *For Sizes B and C, follow the different thread quantities in the end groupings.*
17 Work the rest of the kvalesaum in the red wool.
❕ *For Sizes B and C, follow the different thread quantities in the end groupings.*

construction
❕ *Seam allowance of 1.5 cm (⅝ in) is used throughout, except where otherwise indicated.*

neck and collar
1 Staystitch the neck edges, 1.3 cm (½ in) from the raw edge, on the front and back shirt pieces.
2 With right sides together, sew the darts on the front pieces. Press the darts down.
3 With right sides together, sew the shirt fronts and back together at the shoulder seams. Trim the seam allowances to 1cm (⅜ in), and serge, overlock or zig-zag the seam allowances together. Press the seam allowances to the back.
4 Trim the seam allowance on the lower edge of the collar to 1.5 cm (⅝ in).

57

5 With right side up, sew through both layers of the collar 1 mm (¹⁄₁₆ in) away from the embroidery's lower edge.
6 For the front plackets of the shirt, on each of the shirt fronts, fold 1 cm (⅜ in) hem to the back. Press.
7 Matching the centre of the collar to the centre back, and the collar ends to the same distance away from the placket fold on each side (they should be somewhere near the shirt centre front) pin the collar to the shirt body. Baste it in place.
8 With right sides together, fold the front opening hems back against themselves along the shirt front edge line. Keep the previous 1 cm (⅜ in) fold in place.
9 With the back of the collar uppermost, start at the folded front edge and sew on the seam line (on top of the previous sewing line), to the far end, finishing by sewing across the other front folds.
10 Trim the seam allowance to 7 mm (¼ in).
11 With the collar uppermost, pin the bias tape along the neck seam, matching the raw edge to the trimmed seam allowance. Trim the ends so that they extend about 1 cm (⅜ in) past the end of the collar. Pin then baste in place. Turn it over to the front of the collar so that the seam line is visible. Stitch exactly along the seam line again.
12 Within the seam allowance, carefully clip the collar fabric to give ease. Fold the bias strip over the seam allowance, to wrap it closely. Fold the enclosed seam allowance down against the body of the shirt. Pin then baste in place.
13 Turn the shirt plackets right side out, and down over the bias covered seam allowance.
14 Turn over to the right side and top stitch 6 mm (¼ in) from the collar seam, shirt front edge to shirt front edge.

sleeves

1 Fold the cuff in half along the length. Fold up 1.5 cm (⅝ in) along one of the long edges.
2 Sew across the folded cuff ends.
3 Turn the cuff right way out, keeping the fold in place.
4 Serge, overlock or zig-zag the sleeve seam allowances, without trimming any off.
5 Sew the side seam of the sleeve to 7 cm (2¾ in) from the cuff seam. Press the seam allowances open.
6 At the cuff opening, fold the seam allowance, in half then half again. Starting at the cuff/sleeve seam, top stitch in place 4 mm (³⁄₁₆ in) from the edge of the hem, down one side of the opening, across the seam, then back along the other side, finishing at the cuff/sleeve seam.
7 With right sides together, match the unfolded side of the cuff to the end of the sleeve. Sew them together.

8 Fold the seam allowance up into the cuff and neatly hand stitch the back of the cuff to the seam line.

bodice

1 With right sides together, stitch the bodice side seams. Press the seam allowances open. Serge, overlock or zig-zag the seam allowances.
2 At the bottom of the shirt, fold up 1 cm (⅜ in) to begin the shirt hem.
3 At the bottom of the front plackets, fold 1 cm (⅜ in) to the back. With right sides together, fold the front placket hems back against themselves along the shirt front edge line. Keep the previous 1 cm (⅜ in) fold in place.
4 Sew across the bottom of the front placket folds, 1 cm from the bottom edge.
5 Turn the front plackets right way out.
6 Turning the plackets right way out will have folded another 1 cm (⅜ in) up for the hem within the placket. Continue this 1 cm (⅜ in) fold along the bottom of the shirt to create the hem. Baste in place.
7 Top stitch the hem 8 mm (⁵⁄₁₆ in) from the edge.
8 Sew the front plackets down the front of the shirt, 2.5 cm (1 in) from the front edge.

inserting the sleeves

1 With right sides together, match the sleeve seam to the bodice side seam; pin. Match the dot at the top of the sleeve head to the shoulder seam; pin. Match the notches; pin. Between the notches and the shoulder seam, ease the extra into the available space, pinning regularly. Baste, then stitch the seam.
2 Stitch the under-arm part of the seam between the notches again, just beside the first seam, within the seam allowance.
3 Trim the seam allowance to 7 mm (⅜ in). Serge, overlock or zig-zag the seam allowances.

buttonholes and buttons

1 On the front edge of the sleeve cuffs, measure 3 cm (1³⁄₁₆ in) from the lower edge, and 1 cm (⅜ in) from the end of the cuff. This marks the end of the buttonhole position. Work the buttonholes parallel with the lower edge of the sleeve.
2 Stitch buttons in the corresponding places on the other edge of the sleeves.
3 Following the markings on the pattern, work six buttonholes down the front right (as if being worn) shirt edge.
4 Stitch buttons in the corresponding places on the left shirt edge.
5 Remove all tacking from the garment.

A,D centre
See next column
B,C centre
A
B D
C

D
C A
B
A,D centre
See previous column
B,C centre

framed square

This panel can be worked either as monochrome or in multiple colours by adding the second layer of colours in satin stitch.

size 13.2 x 13.2 cm / 5¼ x 5¼ in
design thread dimensions 146 (w) x 147(h) threads
materials and equipment
- 35 x 35 cm (14 x 14 in) 28 count linen, white
- 2 skeins Au Ver à Soie, Soie d'Alger, 4106
- 1 skein each of Au Ver à Soie, Soie d'Alger 2756, 2931, 4541
- No 24 tapestry needle
- No 24 chenille needle
- laying tool
- 20 cm (8 in) hoop

embroidery

❶ *Follow the chart for stitch and colour placement.*

1 Measure in 11cm (4⁵⁄₁₆ in) from two adjacent sides. Where the measurements meet is the starting point.
2 Mount the embroidery into a hoop so that it is drum tight.
3 Work the black in running stitch with two strands of black silk, using the tapestry needle. Use the laying tool for accurate placement of the threads. Work backstitch turns at the ends of rows.

❶ *If you prefer the monochrome version, you can stop here.*

4 Using the chenille needle and the laying tool, work the coloured stitching using satin stitch and two strands of silk.

❶ *It is traditional to use running stitch for the coloured stitching, but satin stitch raises the stitching a little higher to give a more pronounced effect. If you would prefer yours to be more traditional, use running stitch.*

scissor keep

While stitching some of the projects in this book, I wanted both a tapestry needle and a chenille needle at my fingertips. As I always had my scissors with me I made a scissor keep which is also a mini needlebook. It now goes with everywhere with my needlework projects!

size 3 x 4.5 cm / 1 3/16 x 1 3/4 in
design thread dimensions 96 (w) x 71 (h) threads
materials and equipment

- 15 x 15 cm (6 x 6 in) 40 count linen, cream
- 1 skein Fine d'Aubusson wool, 4002
- 10 m each of Mora wool, 2013, 2061
- No 24 tapestry needle
- No 9 embroidery needle
- 12.5 cm (5 in) hoop
- 3 cm (1 3/16 in) hat elastic, cream
- 8 mm (5/16 in) shank button, cream

- 8.5 x 6.5 cm (3⅜ x 2⁹⁄₁₆ in) doctor's flannel, cream
- machine-sewing thread, cream
- plastic banking or membership card

embroidery

❶ *All embroidery uses the tapestry needle. Follow the chart for stitch and colour placement.*

1 From the top left corner of the linen, measure across 4.5 cm (1¾ in). From this point, measure down 5 cm (2 in). This is the starting point for the top left corner.

2 Mount the fabric in a hoop so that it is drum tight.

3 Work the left section of the embroidery, changing colours as required by the chart. Work the right section of the embroidery similarly.

❶ *Do not continue the threads right across between the two sections. The distance is too long for carrying threads.*

construction

1 From the apricot wool cut two lengths of 40 cm (16 in) and two of 20 cm (8 in). Cut a length of 30 cm (12 in).

2 Lay the two 20 cm (8 in) pieces of wool along the length of the banking card.

3 From the apricot skein, wind the wool around the short width of the banking card, over the two laid lengths, until there is enough fullness to create a good tassel.

4 Keeping the wraps as stable as possible, slide them off the banking card, keeping the two lengths inside.

5 Take the paired ends of the lengths, and twist each pair separately in a clockwise direction, until they are very twisted. Bring the ends together, and let them twist together. Knot the end of the cord.

6 Lay one end of the 30 cm (12 in) length of wool up the tassel from the bottom, and then make a loop at the top. Wrap the wool around the tassel about 8 mm (5/16 in) from the top, to tightly bind the tassel and create a cuff. Pass the end of this thread through the loop, and then pull down on the other end of the thread (at the bottom of the tassel), until it is pulled down under the cuff in a basic knot. Pull both ends equally to tighten the knot behind the cuff. Thread the top end into a needle and bury it in the tassel head.

7 Cut the loops at the bottom of the tassel, and trim the tassel length to 4 cm (1½ in).

8 Run a line of tacking down the sides of the panels six threads away from the edges of the embroidery.

9 Trim the embroidery to 16 threads at the ends of the panels, and 21 threads at the sides.

10 Pair the ends together of the two 40 cm (16 in) lengths of wool. Twist the paired ends in a clockwise direction until the thread is very twisted. Bring the ends together to create a twisted cord. Knot the end of the cord.

11 Fold the elastic in half. With the ends outwards, baste a loop in place at the black dot on the pattern, on the line of tacking. The loop should be large enough to go around the button.

12 Fold the twisted cord in half. With the ends outwards, baste the cord in place at the @ symbol on the pattern.

13 With the end outwards, and positioning it so that the cord will be about 2.5 cm (1 in) long, baste the cord of the tassel in place at the * symbol on the pattern.

14 Position the tassel and cord loop centrally so that they do not accidentally get caught in the seam. Place the doctor's flannel over the embroidered panel's front, matching the edges. Baste in place. Turn it over so the back of the embroidered panel is uppermost. Stitch around the edge, one thread away from the embroidery at the top and bottom, and one thread inside the side tacked guides. Leave a 3 cm (1 3/16 in) gap in one side. Clip the corners. Turn the scissor keep right side out. Stitch the gap closed.

15 With the embroidered side up, stitch down the spine of the scissor keep so that it will naturally fold in half.

16 Sew the button on the opposite edge to the elastic loop. Put the button through the loop to close it.

17 Take the wool loop through the scissor handle and then around the entire scissor keep. Tighten the loop.

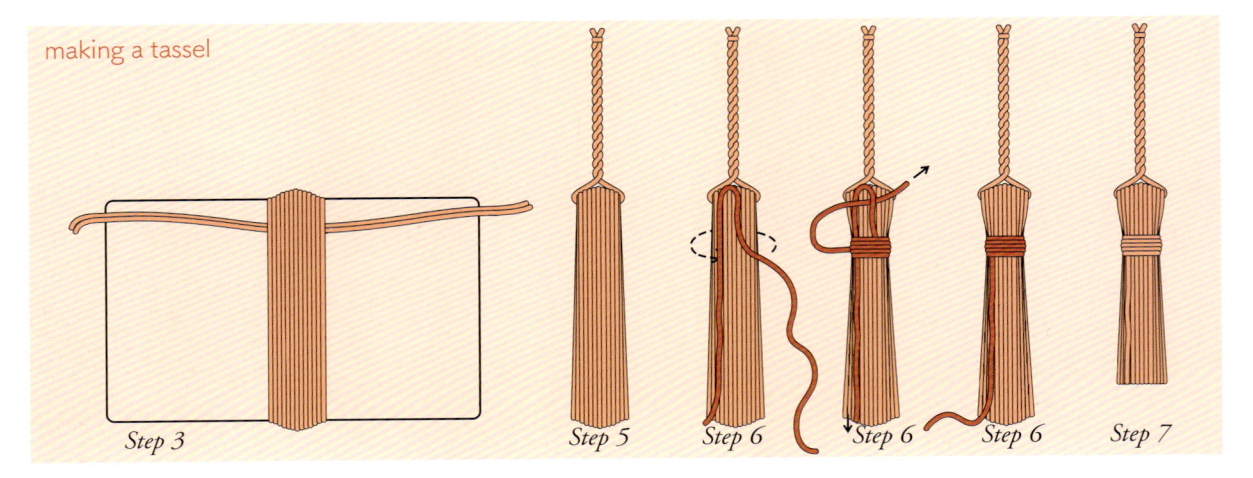

making a tassel

Step 3 Step 5 Step 6 Step 6 Step 6 Step 7

stitches and techniques

left- or right-handed?

Both left- and right-handed stitch instructions are provided in this book. The left-handed instructions are predominantly orange-red, and the right-handed ones are predominantly green. Instructions suitable for both are purple. A tab at the top outer edge of each page indicates the handedness, by colour and an L, R or an L&R.

tacking

Tacking (or basting) the edge of the stitching area or areas is useful preparation for large pieces of smøyg, however, it is often not necessary for small designs such as the pendants or bookmarks.

On larger designs, tacking boundaries around different areas of stitching will give you more freedom of choice in what to stitch next. If all the areas are delineated, you know where everything will go.

Tacking can be counted or not counted. If not counting, simply take stitches of between 5 mm (³⁄₁₆ in) and 10 mm (⅜ in) in length. Counted tacking over and under groups of five threads will more easily relate to the grid on the chart which has thicker grid lines every ten threads.

While the stitch length does not need to be accurate (unless deliberately doing counted tacking) the placement of the tacked lines themselves should be. Otherwise, what is the point of putting them on? With counted embroidery such as pattern darning, accuracy is everything.

counted tacking

Ensure your counted tacking is accurate, or there is no point in counting the tacking at all!

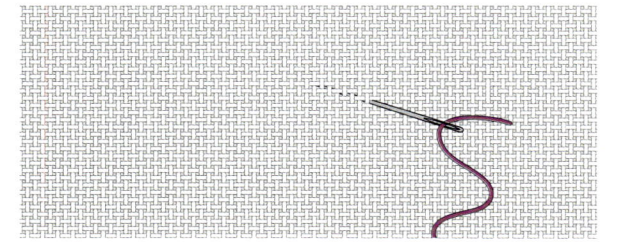

1 The instructions in this book that suggest you put in tacking usually ask you to measure to a specific point. At that specific point, insert your needle.

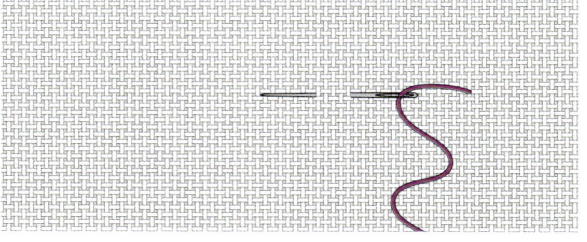

2 Moving in line with the fabric grain (parallel to the fabric threads) count under five threads, and bring the needle back to the front.

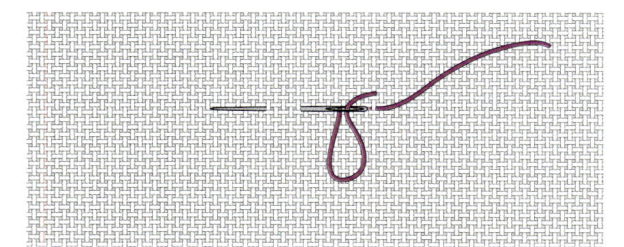

3 Pull the needle and thread through. Insert the needle five threads to the left, and return it to the front five threads further to the left.

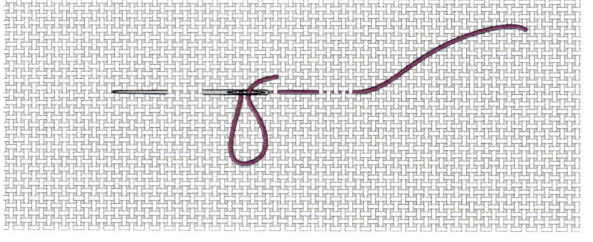

4 Pull the needle and thread through. Insert the needle five threads to the left, and return it to the front five threads further to the left.

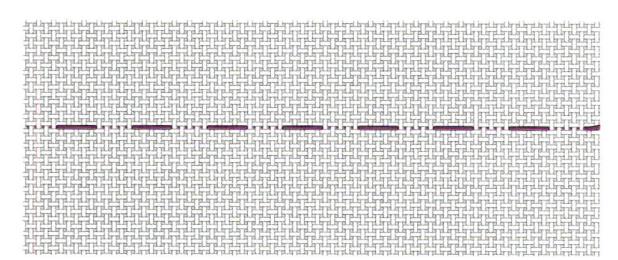

5 Continue in the same way, ensuring all the counting is accurate.

stabbing or sewing?

The main stitch that is used for pattern darning is running stitch. As with most stitches, running stitch can be worked with either a stabbing motion, or a sewing motion.

using a sewing motion

When you stitch using a sewing, scooping or basting motion, insert the needle into the fabric from above and bring it out again further along, before pulling the needle though. It can go in and out a number of times before you pull it through. The needle mostly stays parallel to the surface of the fabric as you stitch. The needle hand stays on top of the surface of the fabric. This method is easier when the fabric is not mounted in an embroidery hoop or on a frame.

using a stabbing motion

When you stitch using a stabbing motion, you insert the needle into the fabric, and pull it through to the other side. To continue, insert the needle from the second side, and pull it through to the first side. There are two distinct movements for the needle to return to the same side as it started. The needle hand moves from one side to the other, or two hands are used with one on top, and the other below. The two hand method requires the fabric to be mounted in a hoop or frame which is on a stand so that the user does not need to hold it. If you use just one hand for the needle, you can hold the hoop or frame in the other one.

which should I use?

Traditionally, smøyg would have been worked in hand, using the sewing method. In the picture shown right, which has been worked with two layers of fabric and shows the back of a collar, we can see that the sewing method has been used. We can tell this because if the stabbing method had been used, we would see all the backs of the stitches on the back. As it is, when the needle has gone up and down through the fabric, it usually hasn't caught the lower layer of fabric. The clear lines of red and green at the edges of the diamonds is where the stitching has changed direction, and therefore the needle has gone all the way through to the back.

However, I use the stabbing method, for pattern darning, with the fabric mounted in a hoop. The reason for this is that when using a sewing motion, it is really easy to pull running stitch too much, thereby making the tension too tight, and narrowing the band of stitching. The stabbing method keeps the fabric flat from the outset, and the stitches sit more happily upon the surface.

I find that when stitching pattern darning with a sewing motion, the thread tends to sit straight and the fabric wiggles on either side of it. It doesn't sit as flat and therefore not as well. Some people improve their results by stitching a line and then pulling the sides of the pattern-darned band outwards at the end of each row, thereby pulling extra thread back into the width of the band, and helping it to sit flatter. This is a little harder to get right when the each line of the stitching is long. It can work reasonably well if the stitching lines are short.

While the pattern darning is best worked in a hoop, the tooth edging and kvalesaum are best worked in hand, with the sewing method. It is more easy to manipulate in the hand, and because the stitching is worked along the folded fabric edge, it does not work well in a hoop.

Although much pattern darning is done with a single strand of thread, at times, two are required to give the proper coverage. When stitching with multiple strands and using a laying tool, the stabbing method gives a far superior result. When using a laying tool, because both hands are in use, you will need to use a stand for your hoop or frame. Alternatively, a hoop or frame half on, half off the table, held down by a weight on the part that is on the table, can also work.

NF.1899-0171

running stitch

Running stitch is the basis for all pattern darning.

Running stitch is often shown worked in horizontal lines, which for left-handers would mean stitching from left to right. When stitching a single line, that makes sense. However, working multiple lines of stitching in succession would mean having to turn the work after each row so that you can again work from left to right. I find it much easier to work vertically, with the lines of stitching running toward you or away from you. This is particularly the case when working with a stab stitching method.

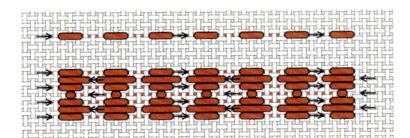

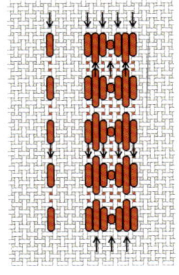

When pattern darning, only change threads at the end of a row. Changing threads halfway through a row interrupts the flow of stitches and may mean the different threads are more obvious. For example, the old thread may be more worn looking than the new thread, and if in the middle of a row, this change will be obvious.

starting a thread

Mount your fabric in a hoop so that it is drum tight.

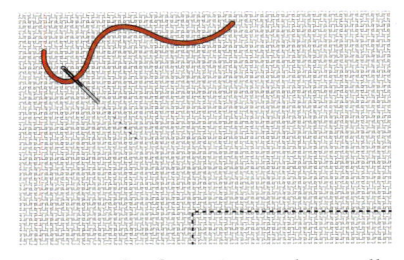

1 From the front, insert the needle in the area surrounding the pattern darning area, about 5 cm (2 in) away from where the stitching needs to start.

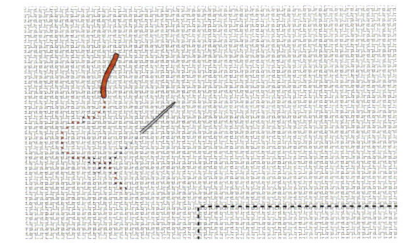

2 Pull the needle through, and leave a tail hanging. Bring the needle back to the front about one third of the way to where the stitching will start.
❶ *The tail will be finished later.*

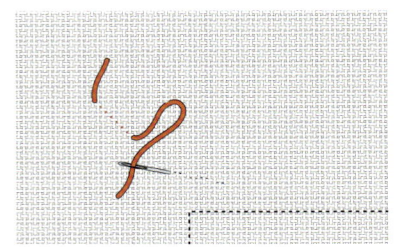

3 Pull the needle through. Insert the needle halfway across the remaining distance to where the stitching will start.

base layer

Where there is more than one layer, or pass, of running stitch, the first layer is the base layer of stitching. Sometimes there is only one layer.

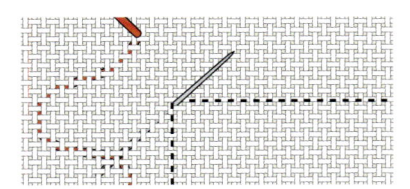

1 Bring the needle out where the stitching needs to begin, at the corner of the stitching area.

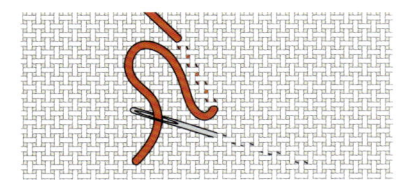

2 Count over the number of threads as required by the chart. Insert the needle.

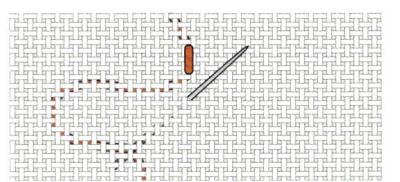

3 Pull the needle and thread through so that the stitch lies gently on the surface of the fabric. Bring the needle back to the front after the number of threads as required by the chart.

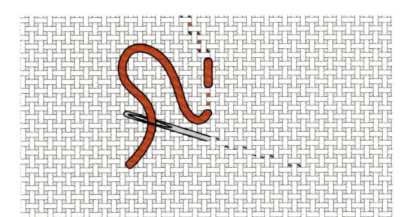

4 Count over the number of threads as required by the chart. Insert the needle.

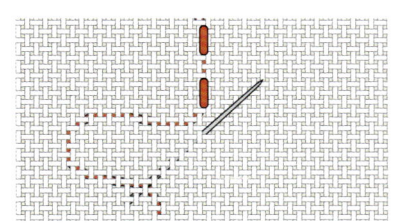

5 Pull the needle and thread through. Bring the needle back to the front after the number of threads as required by the chart.

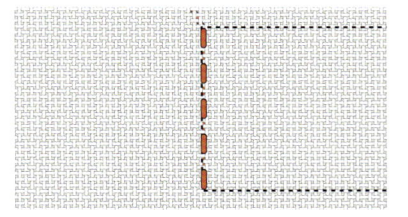

6 Continue in the same manner until you reach the far side of the stitching area.

68

stitch tension

If you choose not to use a hoop, you will need to be particularly careful with your tension. Even with a hoop, do not pull the stitches too tight.

If you pull too tight, the thread will lie straight and the fabric will curve above the stitches on the back, and below the stitches on the surface.

Instead, the fabric should lie straight and the thread will wiggle above and below it, lying on the surface of the fabric.

row ends
Depending on the pattern you are using, there are different ways to work row ends.

simple turn

A simple turn sometimes works and sometimes does not. It all has to do with how the stitches interact with the fabric weave.

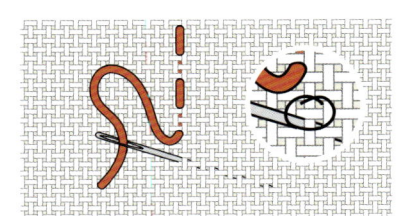

1 Insert the needle at the row end.
❶ *The last fabric thread that you go over must lie horizontally over the thread between this row and the next.*

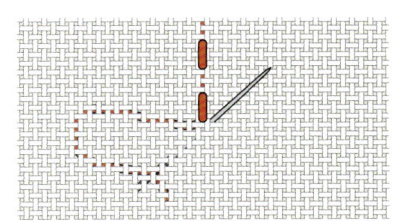

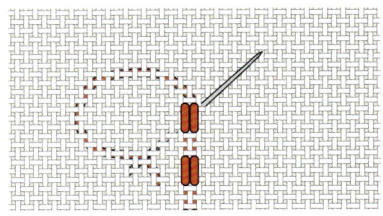

2 Pull the needle and thread through. Bring the needle out one thread to the right.

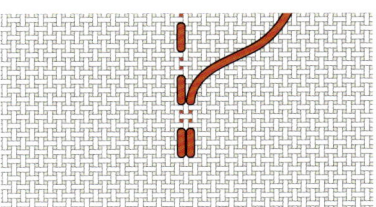

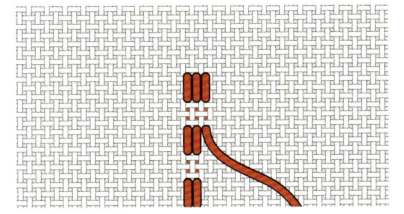

3 Pull the needle through and continue stitching.

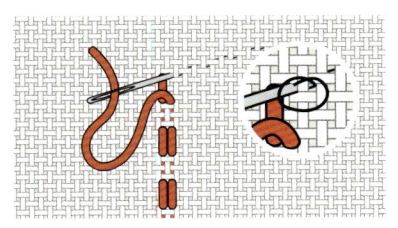

4 At the end of the row, insert the needle.
❶ *The last fabric thread that you go over must lie horizontally over the thread between this row and the next.*

5 Pull the needle and thread through. Bring the needle out one thread to the right.

6 Pull the needle through and continue stitching.

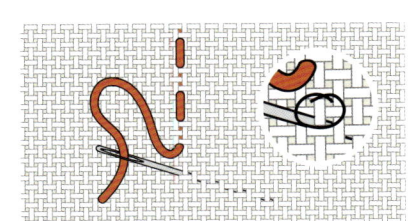

❶ *If the last fabric thread you go over lies horizontally under the thread between this row and the next, this is where problems can be found.*

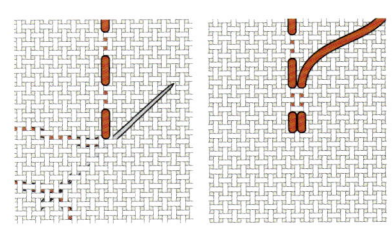

❶ *When starting the new row, the fabric thread will not hold the stitch in place properly, and it will slip back, making both stitches one thread too short.*

❶ *When the simple turn doesn't work, you will need to use a backstitch turn instead.*

❶ *For simple turns to work at both ends, you need a pattern spanning an even number of threads; however, most span an odd number.*

69

backstitch turn

When simple turns do not work at both ends, use backstitch turns at both ends. While you could do a simple turn at one end, and a backstitch turn at the other, it will look more even if you do backstitch turns for both.

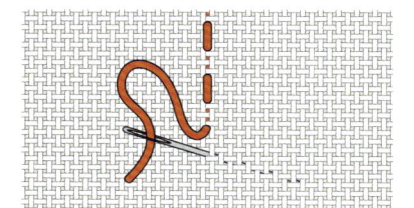

1 Insert the needle at the row end.

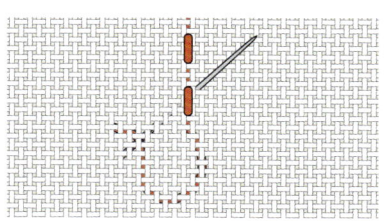

2 Pull the needle and thread through. Insert the needle in the next row, at the far end of the first stitch.
❶ *This stitch will be worked backwards toward the row end.*

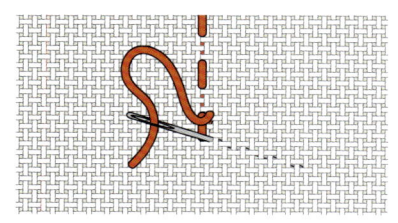

3 Pull the needle and thread through. Insert the needle in the end of the current row.
❶ *Don't pull the end stitch too tight as it pulls the end of the row in. Use loose tension on the end stitches.*

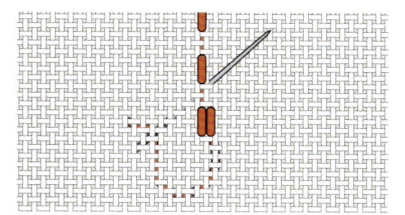

4 Pull the needle and thread through. Bring the needle out for the next stitch.
❶ *Don't pull the end stitch too tight as it pulls the end of the row in. Use loose tension on the end stitches.*

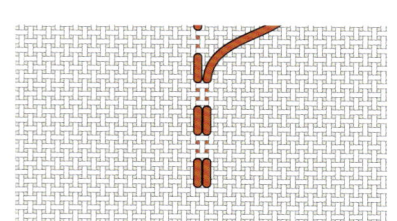

5 Pull the needle through and continue stitching.

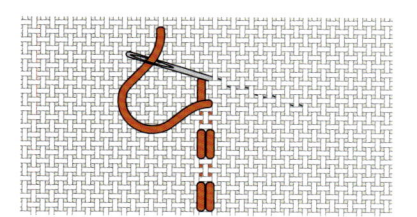

6 At the end of the row, insert the needle.

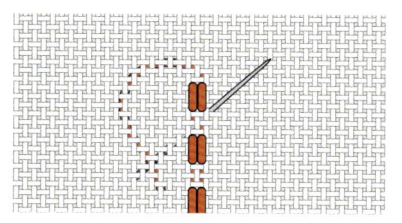

7 Pull the needle and thread through. Insert the needle in the next row, at the far end of the first stitch.
❶ *This stitch will be worked backwards toward the row end.*

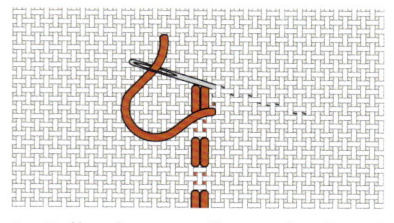

8 Pull the needle and thread through. Insert the needle in the end of the current row.
❶ *Don't pull the end stitch too tight as it pulls the end of the row in. Use loose tension on the end stitches.*

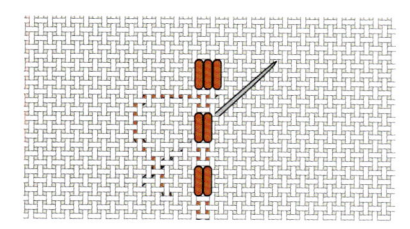

9 Pull the needle and thread through. Bring the needle out for the next stitch.
❶ *Don't pull the end stitch too tight as it pulls the end of the row in. Use loose tension on the end stitches.*

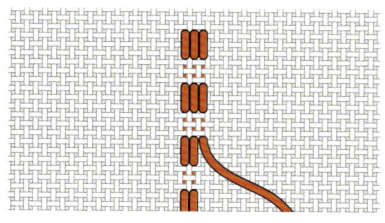

10 Pull the needle through and continue stitching.

❶ *As a simple turn's stitches sit differently than a backstitch turn, use a backstitch turn at both ends so they look the same. This picture shows the back of a piece with backstitch turns at both row ends.*

stepped turn

When the row ends are not level with each other, it is a stepped turn. Row ends step in or out from the previous row, in an adjacent hole or further. This turn is stable and fabric weave does not affect it. Follow your pattern to know whether the next row steps up or down.

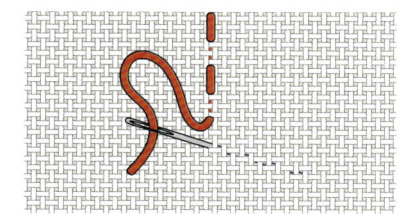

1 Insert the needle at the row end.

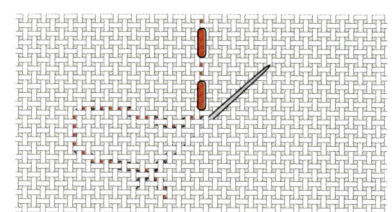

2 Pull the needle and thread through. Bring the needle out one thread down and to the right.

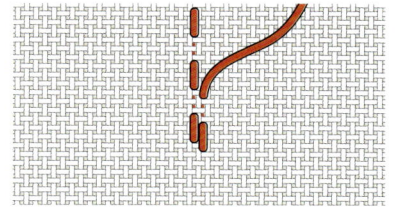

3 Pull the needle through and continue stitching.

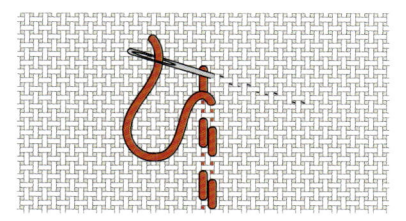

4 At the end of the row, insert the needle.

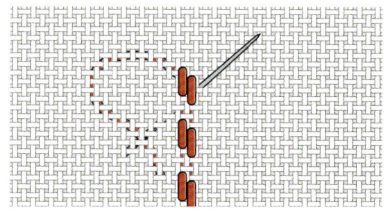

5 Pull the needle and thread through. Bring the needle out one thread down and to the right.

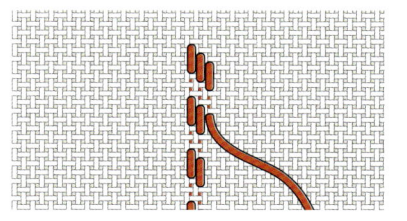

6 Pull the needle through and continue stitching.

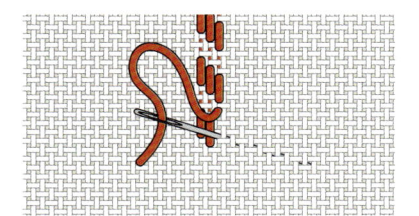

7 At the end of the row, insert the needle.

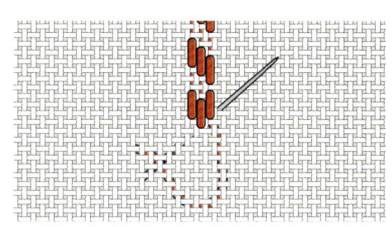

8 Pull the needle and thread through. Bring the needle out one thread up and to the right. Continue stitching.

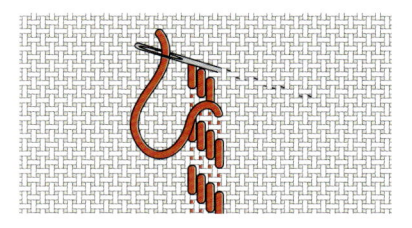

9 At the end of the row, insert the needle.

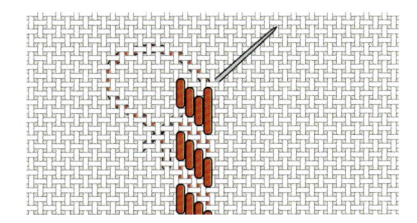

10 Pull the needle and thread through. Bring the needle out one thread up and to the right. Continue stitching.

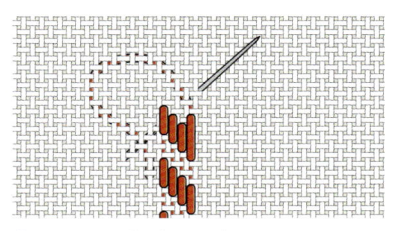

❶ *The needle doesn't have to come out in the next hole up or down. It can jump further, if that's what the pattern requires.*

front border turn

This turn is very stable and is not affected by fabric weave. It is a decorative turn, providing a stitched border along the edge of the design area.

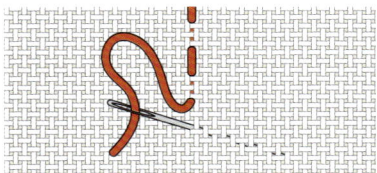

1 Insert the needle at the end of the last running stitch for the row.

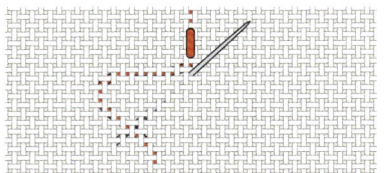

2 Pull the needle and thread through. Bring the needle out two threads further down.

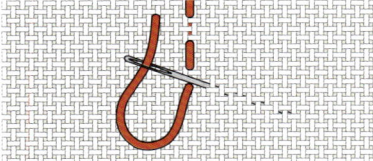

3 Pull the needle and thread through. Insert the needle two threads to the right.
❶ *This creates a border stitch.*

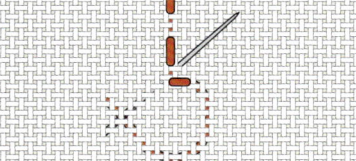

4 Pull the needle and thread through. Bring the needle out one thread to the right of the bottom of the final running stitch of the previous row.

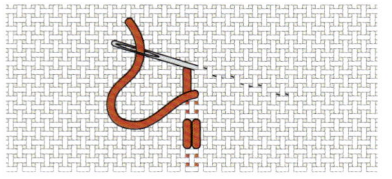

5 Continue stitching as before. At the top of the row, insert the needle for the final running stitch of the row.

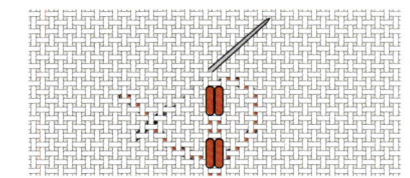

6 Pull the needle and thread through. Bring the needle out two threads up and one to the left.
❶ *The needle comes out above the first row.*

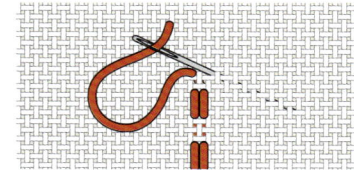

7 Pull the needle and thread through. Insert the needle two threads to the right.
❶ *This creates a border stitch.*

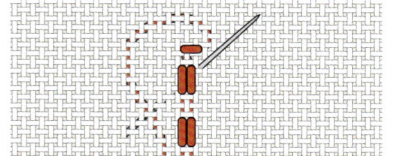

8 Pull the needle and thread through. Bring the needle out two threads down.

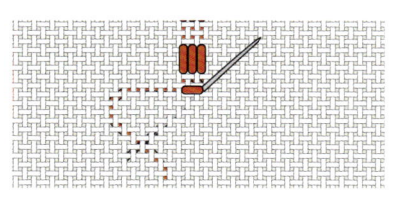

9 Continue stitching. At the end of the row, bring the needle out at the end of the previous border stitch, two threads below the row end.

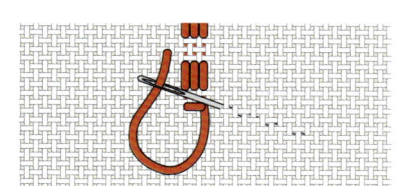

10 Pull the needle and thread through. Insert the needle two threads to the right.

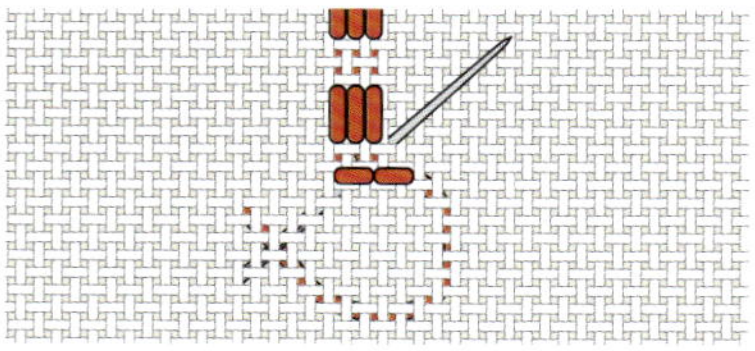

11 Pull the needle through. Bring the needle out one thread to the right of the bottom of the final running stitch of the previous row.

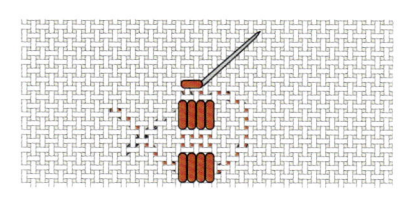

12 Continue stitching. At the row end, bring the needle out at the end of the previous border stitch, two threads above the previous row's end.

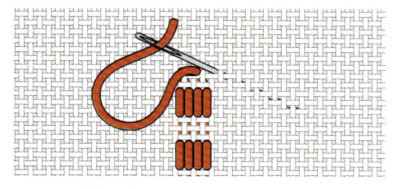

13 Pull the needle and thread through. Insert the needle two threads to the right.

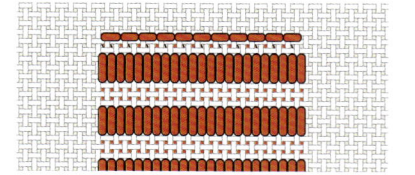

14 Continue stitching.

finishing threads

I use two steps to finish threads when pattern darning. I temporarily park the thread ends so that I can keep stitching, without turning over to the back. At the conclusion of the pattern darning, I turn over to the back to finish off all the thread ends, including the parked beginning ends.

finishing with a parked thread

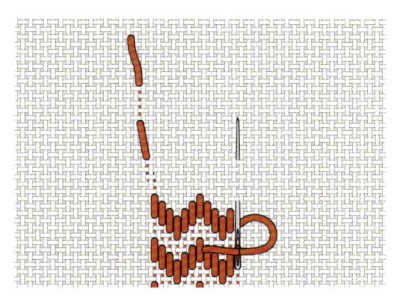

1 Finish stitching at the end of a row. Bring the needle out a short distance away from the end of the row.
❶ *Never change threads in the middle of a row.*

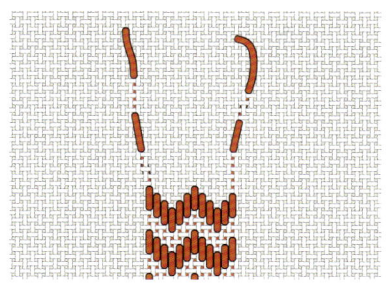

2 Take another long running stitch away from the end of the row. Finish with the thread at the front.
❶ *When the thread remains on the front, you can keep track of it better (ensuring it doesn't get caught up in stitching) than if it were on the back.*

3 Start the next thread (shown as a different colour for illustrative purposes only) similarly.
❶ *Unless it will cause the row ends to work badly, start the new thread at the opposite edge, to keep the thread ends away from each other.*

finishing the parked threads

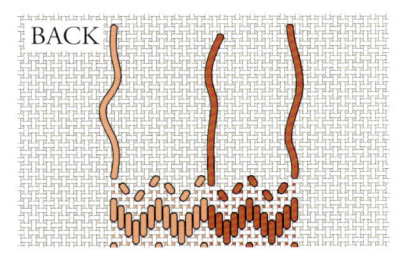

1 Turn the work over to the back and undo all the parked thread ends back to the edge of the pattern darning area.

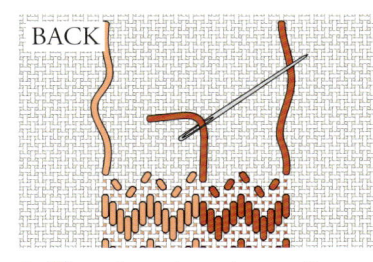

2 Thread one into the needle.

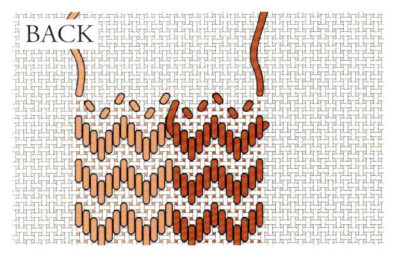

3 Where there is a "channel" of the same colour nearby that you can run the thread under, run it under about 1–2 cm (⅜–¾ in) worth of stitching. Trim the excess.

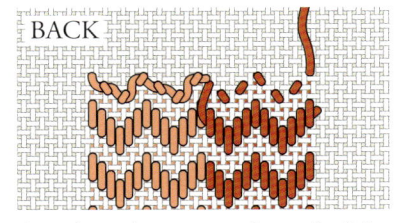

4 Where there is no channel of the same colour, run the thread under the stitch turns at the ends of the rows, like whipped or interlaced running stitch, for about 1–2 cm (⅜–¾ in). Trim the excess.

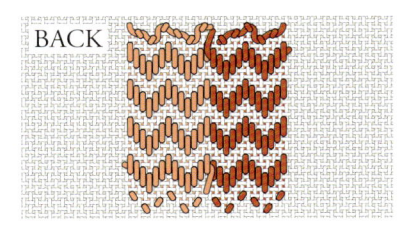

5 Finish all ends.

❶ *Do not use parked threads if the thread being used has an unstable dye. For example, some brightly or strongly coloured threads can leave colour behind in the weave of the fabric if stitches are removed subsequent to stitching. This would leave behind marks well outside the stitching area. In this case, start and finish threads in the back of existing stitching.*

73

top layer

After working the base layer of running stitch, sometimes gaps are filled in with more running stitch: the top layer of running stitch.

Of the two examples, the one on the left shows one colour of stitching (green) surrounded by the stitching of another colour (red). The base layer running stitches continue behind where the top layer sits. In this situation, it is best to use a chenille needle, to come up through the base layer of running stitches, deliberately splitting them. A tapestry needle would make it harder to do this, and the stitches would be more likely to slip beside the previous ones, causing the stitches to sit crooked or out of line.

The example above right shows a top layer (brown) between two sections of base layer stitching (orange and green). The base layer rows end with a gap between the two base layer sections. The stitches do not continue behind the gap. Because of this, either a tapestry needle or a chenille needle can be used for this top layer stitching, as the previous stitches do not need to be split.

starting a thread

Starting this way means there is no need to turn over to the back of the work, which means it is quicker. Alternatively, a thread can also be started by running it under the stitching on the back of the work. A corner is often a good place to start the top layer of running stitch.

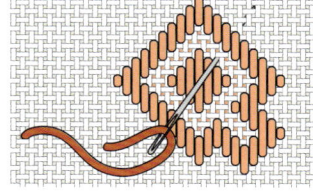

1 From the front, insert the needle in the channel that is to be stitched, about 1–2 cm (⅜–¾ in) from where the top layer stitching will start.
❶ *We will start in the left corner.*

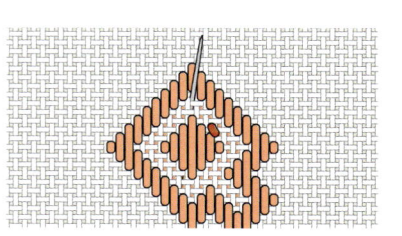

2 Bring the needle out further along the channel. Pull the needle through so that only a short tail shows on the front.
❶ *The tail can be trimmed further later.*

❶ *As you start stitching, these stitches will be covered. Trim the tail if it is too long when the stitching gets close to it.*

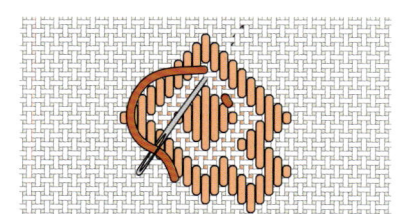

3 Insert the needle either one thread above or below where it emerged.
❶ *This will create a tiny stitch on the front. By inserting above or below, the stitch stays in line with the running stitches that will soon cover it, meaning it won't show.*

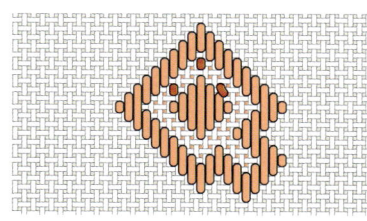

4 Repeat this tiny stitch further along the channel, closer to where the top layer stitching will start.
❶ *Always make sure the tiny stitches sit vertically, so that they will be covered by the subsequent stitches.*

top layer in gap between base layer sections

When the base layer stitching sections have a gap between them the top layer stitching is simply worked in regular running stitch. The previous row end stitches do not need to be split, so a tapestry needle can be used.

top layer over base layer

When the base layer stitching goes behind the channel where top layer stitching will be worked, you will need to split the ends of the base layer stitches when you bring the needle out and insert it.

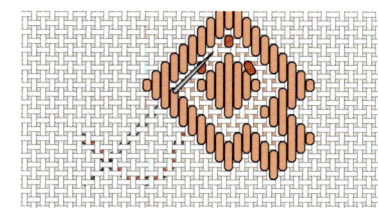

1 Bring the needle out at the bottom end of the first stitch position, splitting the base layer stitch's end.
❶ *Split the base layer stitch or the top layer stitch will sit out of line.*

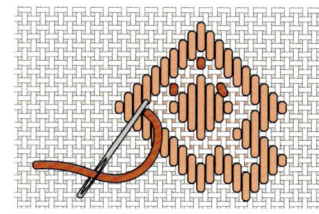

2 Pull the needle through. Insert it one thread up, splitting the end of the base layer stitch.

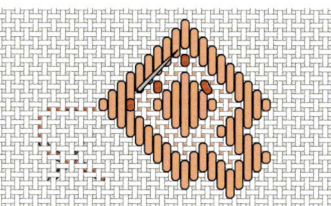

3 Pull the needle through. Bring it out through the end of the adjacent stitch, splitting the end of the base layer stitch.

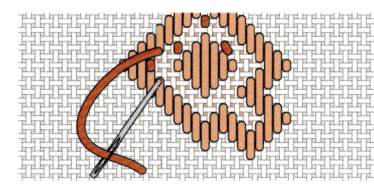

4 Pull the needle through. Insert it three threads down, splitting the end of the next base layer running stitch.

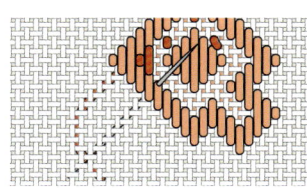

5 Pull the needle through. Bring it out through the end of the next stitch, splitting the base layer stitch's end.

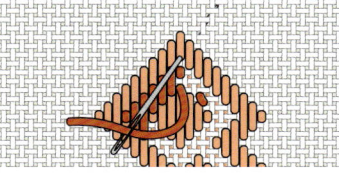

6 Stitch up the channel, completing the side by inserting the needle at the top of the uppermost stitch.

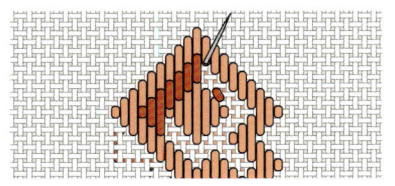

7 Pull the needle through. Bring it out through the end of the next stitch, splitting the base layer stitch's end.

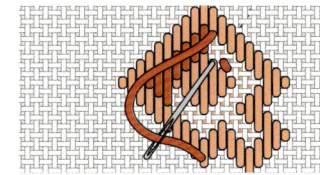

8 Pull the needle through. Insert it three threads down, splitting the end of the next base layer stitch.

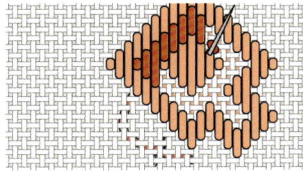

9 Pull the needle through. Bring it out through the end of the next stitch, splitting the base layer stitch's end.

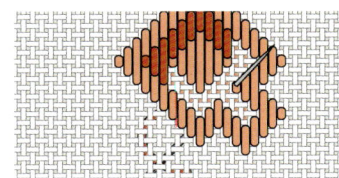

10 Continue stitching. Bring the needle out at the bottom of the space for the longest of the corner stitches.

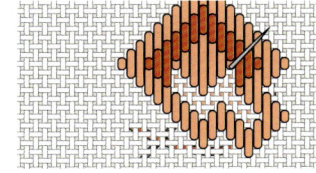

11 Complete the three stitches of the corner. Bring the needle out at the top of the next stitch along the path.

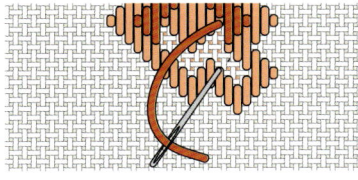

12 Pull the needle through. Insert it five threads down, splitting the end of the base layer stitch.

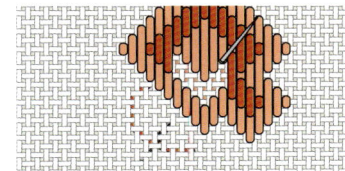

13 Complete the side path. Bring the needle out at the top of the space for the next stitch across, splitting the end of the base layer stitch.

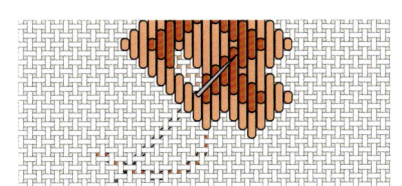

14 Complete the side, then bring the needle out through the end of the next stitch, splitting the base layer stitch's end.

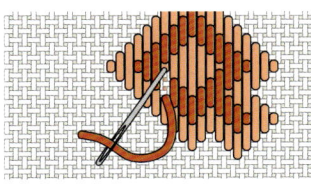

15 Keep stitching up the channel, finishing by inserting the needle at the last stitch's top. On the back, finish by running the thread under the stitches.

running stitch

Running stitch is the basis for all pattern darning.

Running stitch is often shown worked in horizontal lines, which for right-handers would mean stitching from right to left. When stitching a single line, that makes sense. However, working multiple lines of stitching in succession would mean having to turn the work after each row so that you can again work from right to left. I find it much easier to work vertically, with the lines of stitching running toward you or away from you. This is particularly the case when working with a stab stitching method.

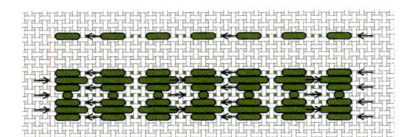

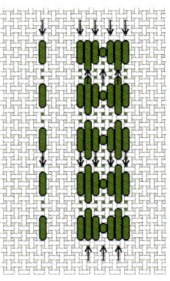

When pattern darning, only change threads at the end of a row. Changing threads halfway through a row interrupts the flow of stitches and may mean the different threads are more obvious. For example, the old thread may be more worn looking than the new thread, and if in the middle of a row, this change will be obvious.

starting a thread

Mount your fabric in a hoop so that it is drum tight.

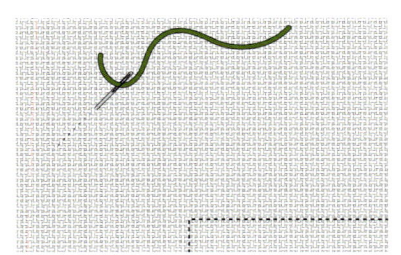

1 From the front, insert the needle in the area surrounding the pattern darning area, about 5 cm (2 in) away from where the stitching needs to start.

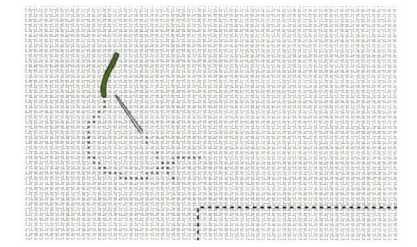

2 Pull the needle through, and leave a tail hanging. Bring the needle back to the front about one third of the way to where the stitching will start.
❶ *The tail will be finished later.*

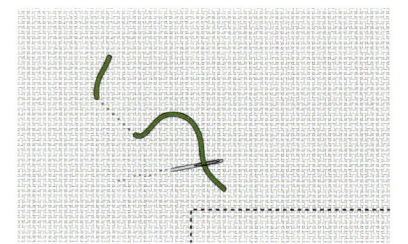

3 Pull the needle through. Insert the needle halfway across the remaining distance to where the stitching will start.

base layer

Where there is more than one layer, or pass, of running stitch, the first layer is the base layer of stitching. Sometimes there is only one layer.

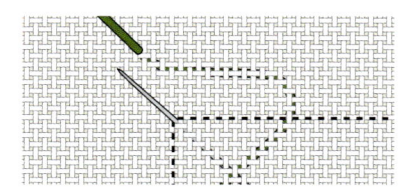

1 Bring the needle out where the stitching needs to begin, at the corner of the stitching area.

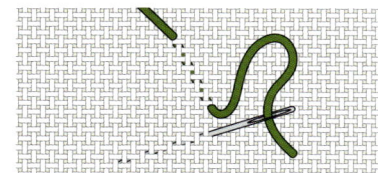

2 Count over the number of threads as required by the chart. Insert the needle.

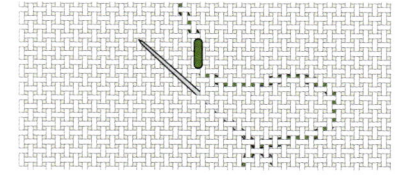

3 Pull the needle and thread through so that the stitch lies gently on the surface of the fabric. Bring the needle back to the front after the number of threads as required by the chart.

4 Count over the number of threads as required by the chart. Insert the needle.

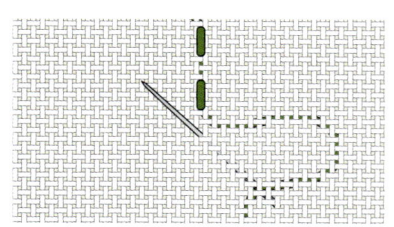

5 Pull the needle and thread through. Bring the needle back to the front after the number of threads as required by the chart.

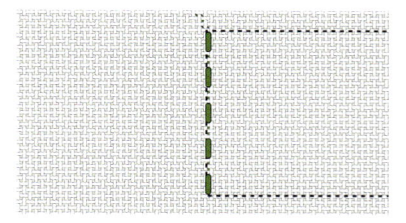

6 Continue in the same manner until you reach the far side of the stitching area.

stitch tension

If you choose not to use a hoop, you will need to be particularly careful with your tension. Even with a hoop, do not pull the stitches too tight.

If you pull too tight, the thread will lie straight and the fabric will curve above the stitches on the back, and below the stitches on the surface.

Instead, the fabric should lie straight and the thread will wiggle above and below it, lying on the surface of the fabric.

row ends Depending on the pattern you are using, there are different ways to work row ends.

simple turn

A simple turn sometimes works and sometimes does not. It all has to do with how the stitches interact with the fabric weave.

1 Insert the needle at the row end.
❶ *The last fabric thread that you go over must lie horizontally over the thread between this row and the next.*

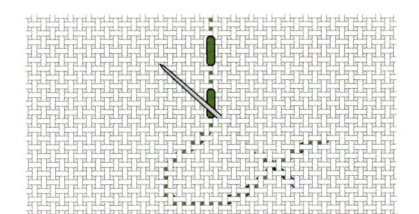

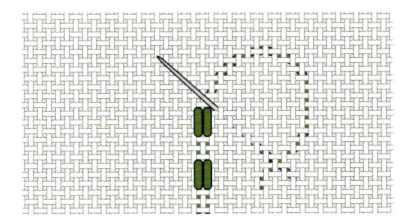

2 Pull the needle and thread through. Bring the needle out one thread to the right.

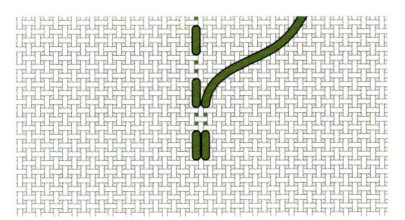

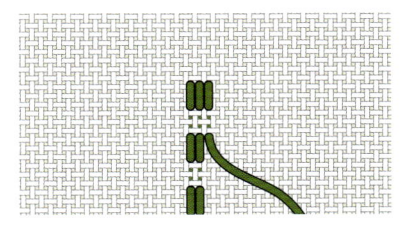

3 Pull the needle through and continue stitching.

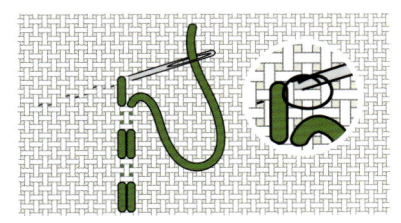

4 At the end of the row, insert the needle.
❶ *The last fabric thread that you go over must lie horizontally over the thread between this row and the next.*

5 Pull the needle and thread through. Bring the needle out one thread to the right.

6 Pull the needle through and continue stitching.

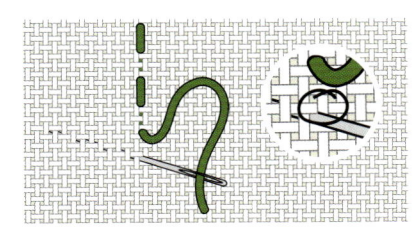

❶ *If the last fabric thread you go over lies horizontally under the thread between this row and the next, this is where problems can be found.*

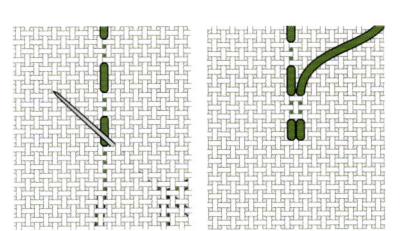

❶ *When starting the new row, the fabric thread will not hold the stitch in place properly, and it will slip back, making both stitches one thread too short.*

❶ *When the simple turn doesn't work, you will need to use a backstitch turn instead.*

❶ *For simple turns to work at both ends, you need a pattern spanning an even number of threads; however, most span an odd number.*

backstitch turn

When simple turns don't work at both ends, use backstitch turns at both ends. While you could do a simple turn at one end, and a backstitch turn at the other, it will look more even if you do backstitch turns for both.

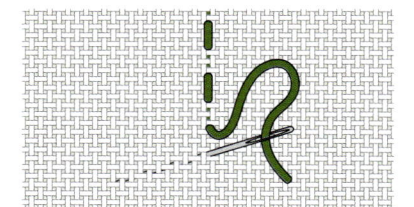

1 Insert the needle at the row end.

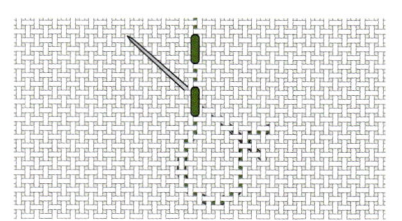

2 Pull the needle and thread through. Insert the needle in the next row, at the far end of the first stitch.
❶ *This stitch will be worked backwards from the far end.*

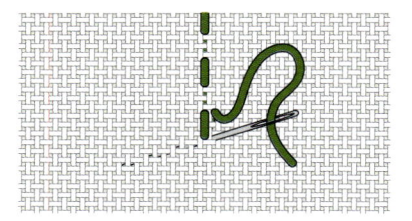

3 Pull the needle and thread through. Insert the needle in the end of the current row.
❶ *Don't pull the end stitch too tight as it pulls the end of the row in. Use loose tension on the end stitches.*

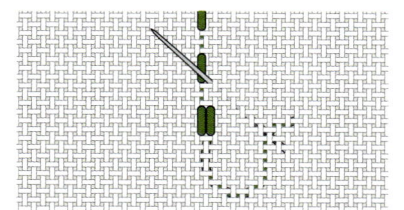

4 Pull the needle and thread through. Bring the needle out for the next stitch.
❶ *Don't pull the end stitch too tight as it pulls the end of the row in. Use loose tension on the end stitches.*

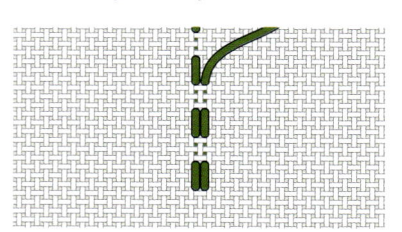

5 Pull the needle through and continue stitching.

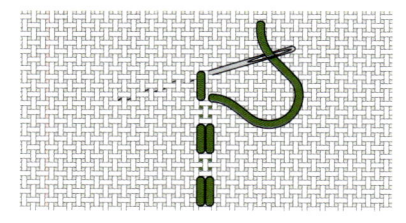

6 At the end of the row, insert the needle.

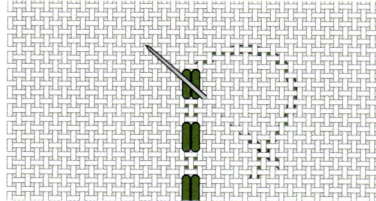

7 Pull the needle and thread through. Insert the needle in the next row, at the far end of the first stitch.
❶ *This stitch will be worked backwards from the far end.*

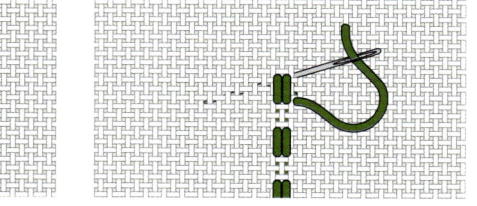

8 Pull the needle and thread through. Insert the needle in the end of the current row.
❶ *Don't pull the end stitch too tight as it pulls the end of the row in. Use loose tension on the end stitches.*

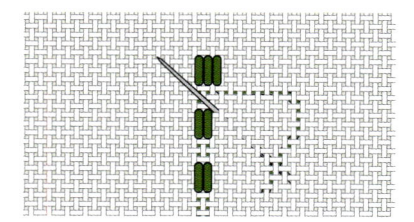

9 Pull the needle and thread through. Bring the needle out for the next stitch.
❶ *Don't pull the end stitch too tight as it pulls the end of the row in. Use loose tension on the end stitches.*

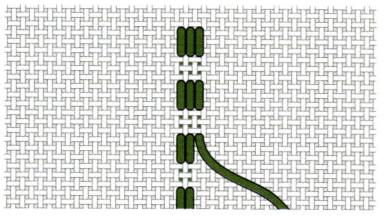

10 Pull the needle through and continue stitching.

❶ *As a simple turn's stitches sit differently than a backstitch turn, you can use a backstitch turn at both ends so they look the same. This picture shows the back of a piece with backstitch turns at both row ends.*

78

stepped turn

When the row ends are not level with each other, it is a stepped turn. Row ends step in or out from the previous row, in an adjacent hole or further. This turn is stable and fabric weave does not affect it. Follow your pattern to know whether the next row steps up or down.

1 Insert the needle at the row end.

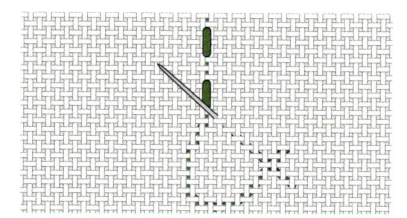

2 Pull the needle and thread through. Bring the needle out one thread down and to the right.

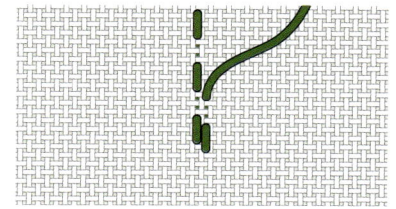

3 Pull the needle through and continue stitching.

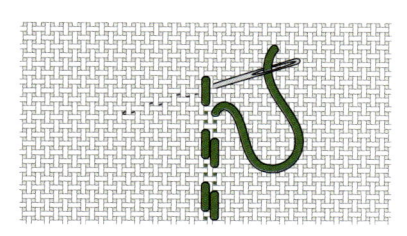

4 At the end of the row, insert the needle.

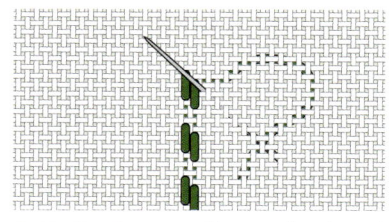

5 Pull the needle and thread through. Bring the needle out one thread down and to the right.

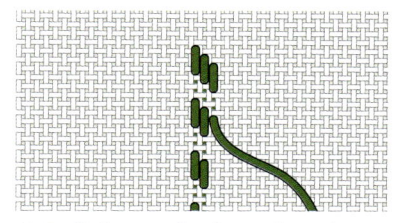

6 Pull the needle through and continue stitching.

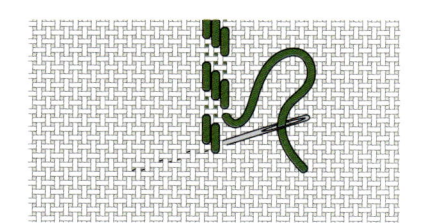

7 At the end of the row, insert the needle.

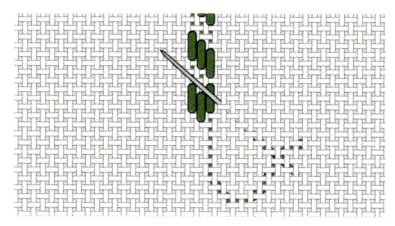

8 Pull the needle and thread through. Bring the needle out one thread up and to the right. Continue stitching.

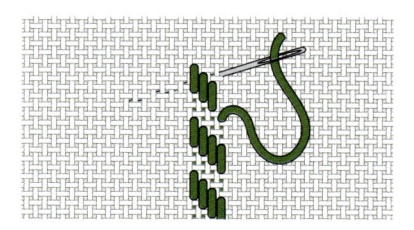

9 At the end of the row, insert the needle.

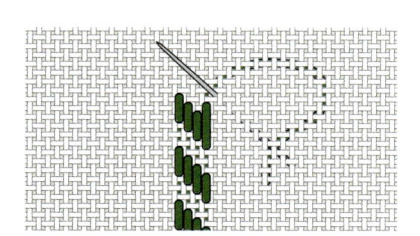

10 Pull the needle and thread through. Bring the needle out one thread up and to the right. Continue stitching.

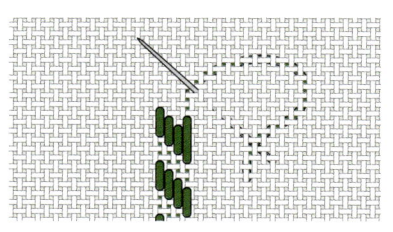

❶ *The needle doesn't have to come out in the next hole up or down. It can jump further, if that's what the pattern requires.*

front border turn

This turn is very stable and is not affected by fabric weave. It is a decorative turn, providing a stitched border along the edge of the design area.

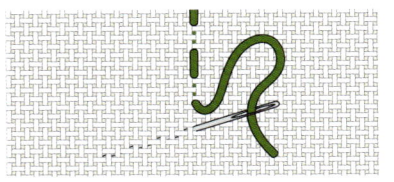

1 Insert the needle at the end of the last running stitch for the row.

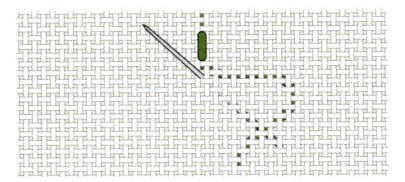

2 Pull the needle and thread through. Bring the needle out two threads further down.

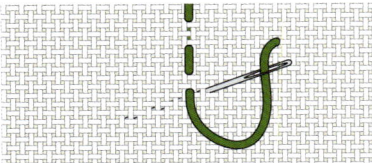

3 Pull the needle and thread through. Insert the needle two threads to the right.
- *This creates a border stitch.*

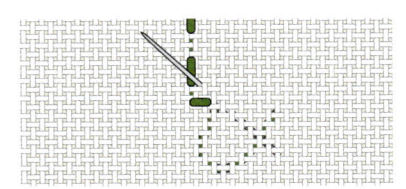

4 Pull the needle and thread through. Bring the needle out one thread to the right of the bottom of the final running stitch of the previous row.

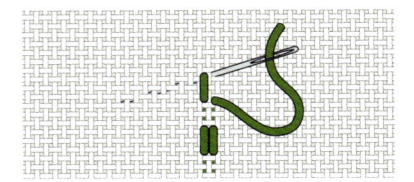

5 Continue stitching as before. At the top of the row, insert the needle for the final running stitch of the row.

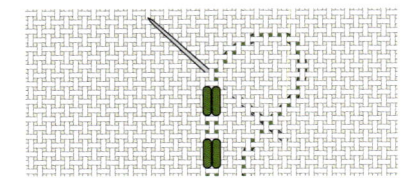

6 Pull the needle and thread through. Bring the needle out two threads up and one to the left.
- *The needle comes out above the first row.*

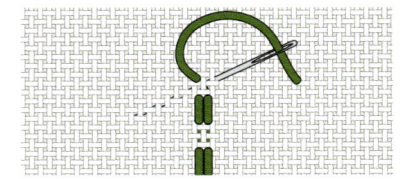

7 Pull the needle and thread through. Insert the needle two threads to the right.
- *This creates a border stitch.*

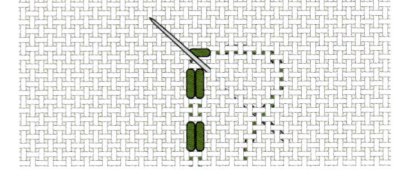

8 Pull the needle and thread through. Bring the needle out two threads down.

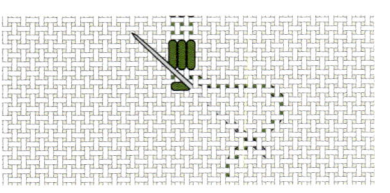

9 Continue stitching. At the end of the row, bring the needle out at the end of the previous border stitch, two threads below the row end.

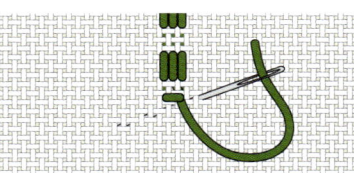

10 Pull the needle and thread through. Insert the needle two threads to the right.

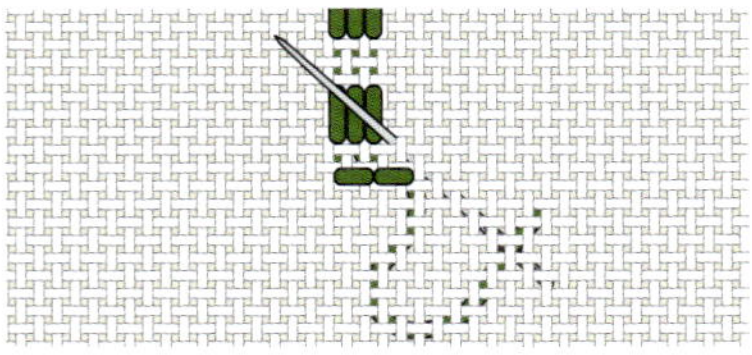

11 Pull the needle through. Bring the needle out one thread to the right of the bottom of the final running stitch of the previous row.

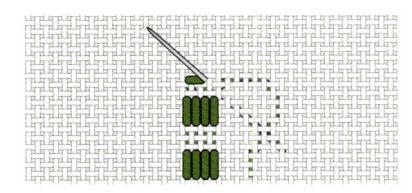

12 Continue stitching. At the row end, bring the needle out at the end of the previous border stitch, two threads above the previous row's end.

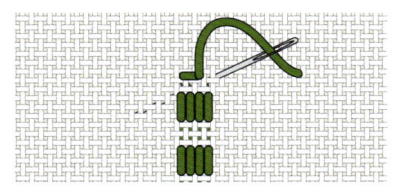

13 Pull the needle and thread through. Insert the needle two threads to the right.

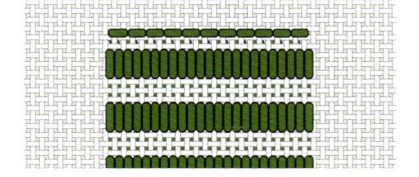

14 Continue stitching.

finishing threads

I use two steps to finish threads when pattern darning. I temporarily park the thread ends so that I can keep stitching, without turning over to the back. At the conclusion of the pattern darning, I turn over to the back to finish off all the thread ends, including the parked beginning ends.

finishing with a parked thread

1 Finish stitching at the end of a row. Bring the needle out a short distance away from the end of the row.
❶ *Never change threads in the middle of a row.*

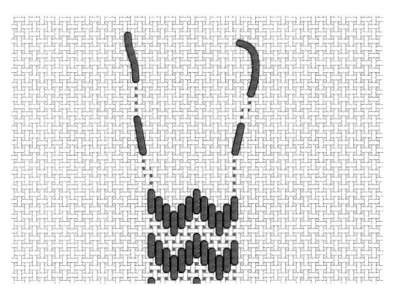

2 Take another long running stitch away from the end of the row. Finish with the thread at the front.
❶ *When the thread remains on the front, you can keep track of it better (ensuring it doesn't get caught up in stitching) than if it were on the back.*

3 Start the next thread (shown as a different colour for illustrative purposes only) similarly.
❶ *Unless it will cause the row ends to work badly, it can help to start the new thread at the opposite edge, to keep the thread ends away from each other.*

finishing the parked threads

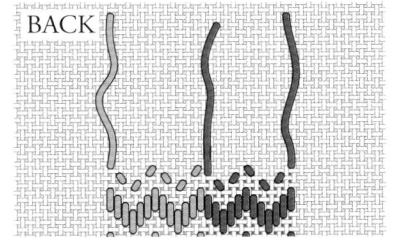

1 Turn the work over to the back and undo all the parked thread ends back to the edge of the pattern darning area.

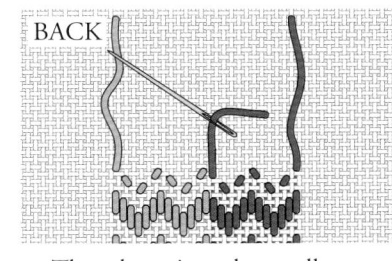

2 Thread one into the needle.

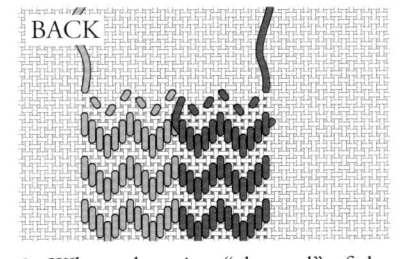

3 Where there is a "channel" of the same colour nearby that you can run the thread under, run it under about 1–2 cm (⅜–¾ in) worth of stitching. Trim the excess.

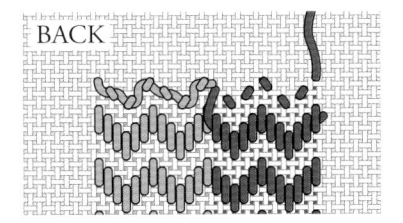

4 Where there is no channel of the same colour, run the thread under the stitch turns at the ends of the rows, like whipped or interlaced running stitch, for about 1–2 cm (⅜–¾ in). Trim the excess.

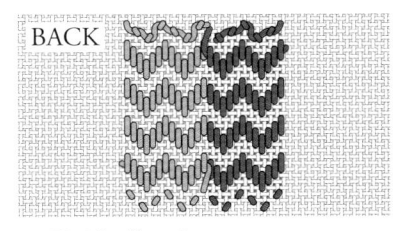

5 Finish all ends.

❶ *Do not use parked threads if the thread being used has an unstable dye. For example, some brightly or strongly coloured threads can leave colour behind in the weave of the fabric if stitches are removed subsequent to stitching. This would leave behind marks well outside the stitching area. In this case, start and finish threads in the back of existing stitching.*

R top layer

After working the base layer of running stitch, sometimes gaps are filled in with more running stitch: the top layer of running stitch.

Of the two examples, the one on the left shows one colour of stitching (green) surrounded by the stitching of another colour (red). The base layer running stitches continue behind where the top layer sits. In this situation, it is best to use a chenille needle, to come up through the base layer of running stitches, deliberately splitting them. A tapestry needle would make it harder to do this, and the stitches would be more likely to slip beside the previous ones, causing the stitches to sit crooked or out of line.

The example above right shows a top layer (brown) between two sections of base layer stitching (orange and green). The base layer rows end with a gap between the two base layer sections. The stitches do not continue behind the gap. Because of this, either a tapestry needle or a chenille needle can be used for this top layer stitching, as the previous stitches do not need to be split.

starting a thread

Starting this way means there is no need to turn over to the back of the work, which means it is quicker. Alternatively, a thread can also be started by running it under the stitching on the back of the work. A corner is often a good place to start the top layer of running stitch.

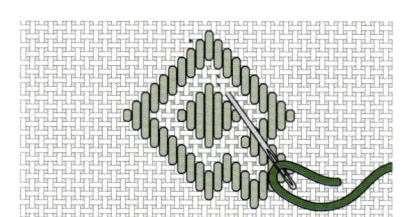

1 From the front, insert the needle in the channel that is to be stitched, about 1–2 cm (⅜–¾ in) from where the top layer stitching will start.
❶ *We will start in the left corner.*

2 Bring the needle out further along the channel. Pull the needle through so that only a short tail shows on the front.
❶ *The tail can be trimmed further later.*

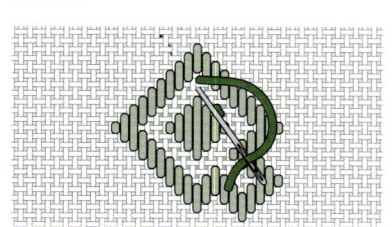

❶ *As you start stitching, these stitches will be covered. Trim the tail if it is too long when the stitching gets close to it.*

3 Insert the needle either one thread above or below where it emerged.
❶ *This will create a tiny stitch on the front. By inserting above or below, the stitch stays in line with the running stitches that will soon cover it, meaning it won't show.*

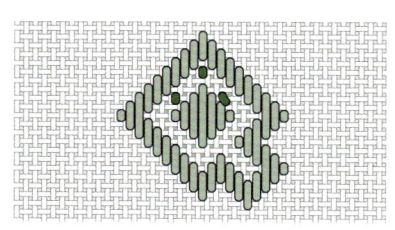

4 Repeat this tiny stitch further along the channel, closer to where the top layer stitching will start.
❶ *Always make sure the tiny stitches sit vertically, so that they will be covered by the subsequent stitches.*

top layer in gap between base layer sections

When the base layer stitching sections have a gap between them the top layer stitching is simply worked in regular running stitch. The previous row end stitches do not need to be split, so a tapestry needle can be used.

top layer over base layer

When the base layer stitching goes behind the channel where top layer stitching will be worked, you will need to split the ends of the base layer stitches when you bring the needle out and insert it.

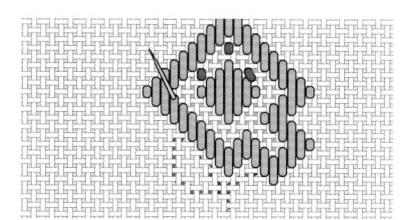

1 Bring the needle out at the bottom end of the first stitch position, splitting the base layer stitch's end.
❶ *Split the base layer stitch or the top layer stitch will sit out of line.*

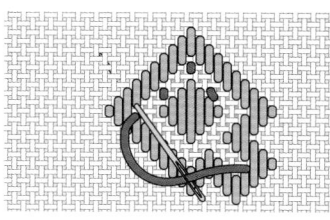

2 Pull the needle through. Insert it one thread up, splitting the end of the base layer stitch.

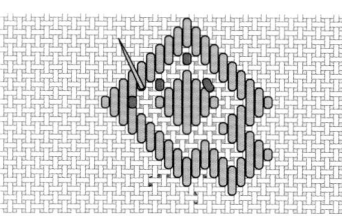

3 Pull the needle through. Bring it out through the end of the adjacent stitch, splitting the end of the base layer stitch.

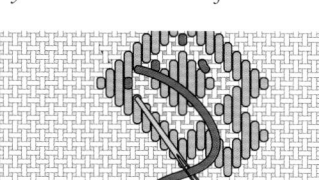

4 Pull the needle through. Insert it three threads down, splitting the end of the next base layer running stitch.

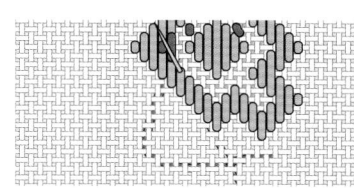

5 Pull the needle through. Bring it out through the end of the next stitch, splitting the base layer stitch's end.

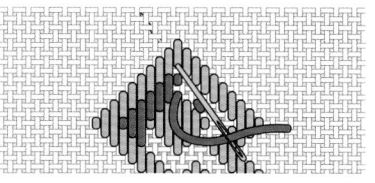

6 Stitch up the channel, completing the side by inserting the needle at the top of the uppermost stitch.

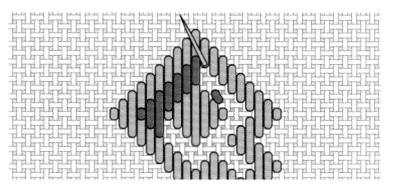

7 Pull the needle through. Bring it out through the end of the next stitch, splitting the base layer stitch's end.

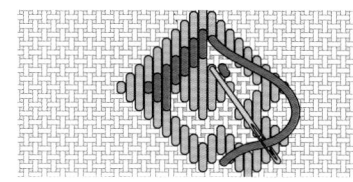

8 Pull the needle through. Insert it three threads down, splitting the end of the next base layer stitch.

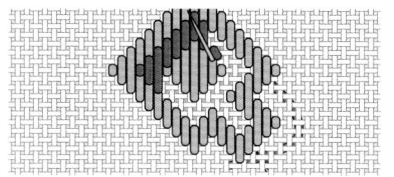

9 Pull the needle through. Bring it out through the end of the next stitch, splitting the base layer stitch's end.

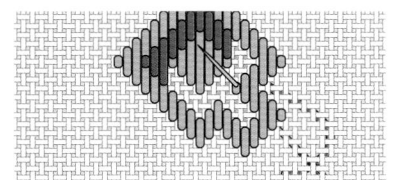

10 Continue stitching. Bring the needle out at the bottom of the space for the longest of the corner stitches.

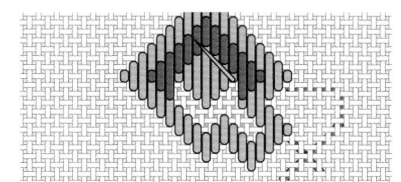

11 Complete the three stitches of the corner. Bring the needle out at the top of the next stitch along the path.

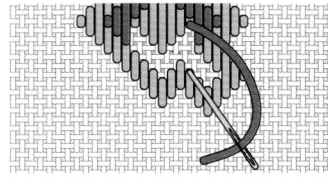

12 Pull the needle through. Insert it five threads down, splitting the end of the base layer stitch.

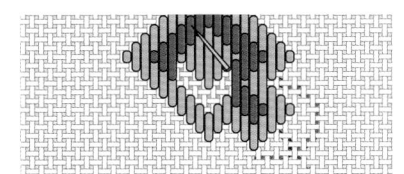

13 Complete the side path. Bring the needle out at the top of the space for the next stitch across, splitting the end of the base layer stitch.

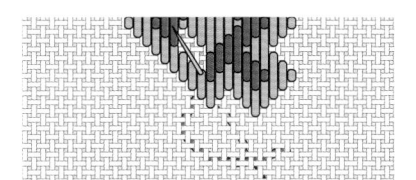

14 Complete the side, then bring the needle out through the end of the next stitch, splitting the base layer stitch's end.

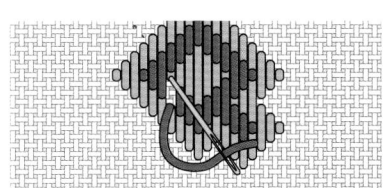

15 Keep stitching up the channel, finishing by inserting the needle at the last stitch's top. On the back, finish by running the thread under the stitches.

using a laying tool

Using a laying tool will help to untwist threads, whether flat silk or multiple thread strands, so that they sit flatter and straighter. By removing the twists, the thread will give better coverage.

A laying tool is a smooth metal, glass or wooden stick with a pointed or rounded end. Tekobaris, trolley needles, stilettos, awls, hatpins, hijab pins, hair sticks, fine double pointed knitting needles and large embroidery needles can all be used as laying tools. Because both hands will be used, mounting the embroidery in a hoop or frame that is on a stand will be advantageous.

A laying tool helps to guide a thread's multiple strands into place so they sit parallel to each other, without twisting (below left, right section) creating a smoother and more uniform finish than twisted threads (below left and right, left sections). When working with flat silk, a laying tool helps the strands to sit wide and flat like a ribbon (below right, right section).

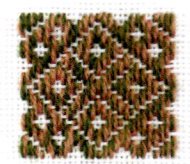

stitching away from yourself with multiple strands

1 Separate all the strands. Bring two of them back together.
❶ *Separating and recombining the strands helps them to intertwine less.*
❶ *These instructions are written for two strands, but more could be used.*

2 Mount the fabric into a hoop or frame so that it is drum tight.
❶ *This allows one hand to be used for the needle, and the other for the laying tool.*

3 Thread two strands of thread into the needle and bring the needle and thread out of the fabric.

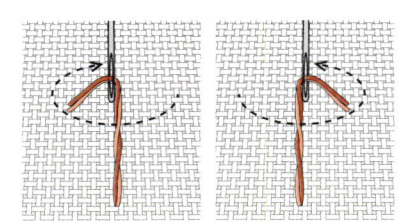

4 Lift up the working thread so that it is perpendicular to the fabric. Twist it either in a clockwise or anticlockwise direction to ensure it is as untwisted as possible.
❶ *This will make the next stitch easier.*

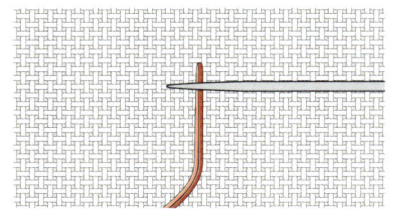

5 Hold the laying tool in your right hand and lay the tip against the untwisted working thread to flatten it downward, back against the fabric.

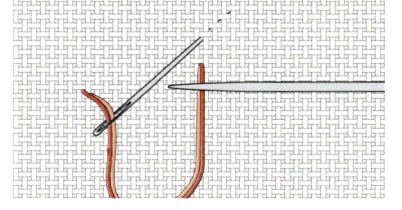

6 Keeping the laying tool in place, insert the needle for the stitch.

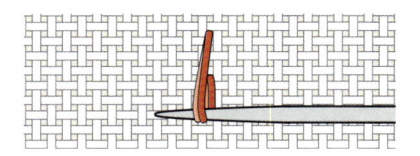

7 Keeping the laying tool in place, pull the needle and thread through until the stitch has no slack between where it enters the fabric and the laying tool.

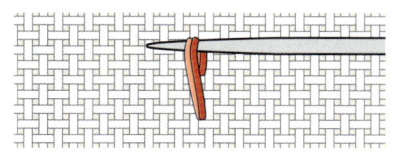

8 Lift the laying tool (keeping the strands untwisted) and gently run it along the inside of the stitch, a little further than the full length of the stitch. Keep tension on the thread as you do this.
❶ *Do not allow the strands to twist.*

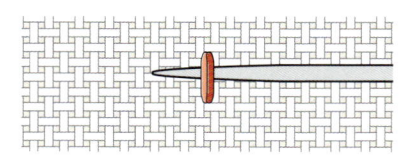

9 Keeping the laying tool in place under the thread, but allowing it to move with the thread, pull the thread through so that the stitch lies flat.
❶ *Keep the strands twist-free between the laying tool and the fabric.*

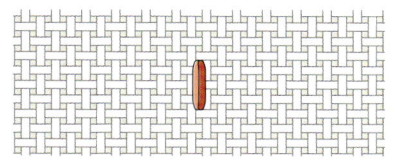

10 Remove the laying tool. The stitch should lie flat with both strands remaining perfectly parallel.

❶ *If the strands twist, insert the laying tool under the stitch. Lift it, sliding and stroking it along the inside of the strands, keeping them twist-free between the laying tool and where they emerged from the fabric. Pull the stitch down into the fabric until there is no twist showing.*

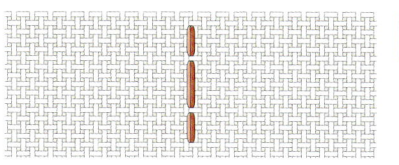

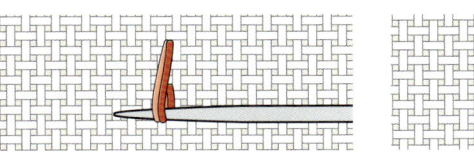

11 Repeat the process for each stitch.
❶ *It may be slow at first, but with practice it will get quicker.*

stitching toward yourself with multiple strands

1 Separate all the strands. Bring two of them back together.
❶ *Separating and recombining the strands helps them to intertwine less.*
❶ *These instructions are written for two strands, but more could be used.*

2 Mount the fabric into a hoop or frame so that it is drum tight.
❶ *This allows one hand to be used for the needle, and the other for the laying tool.*

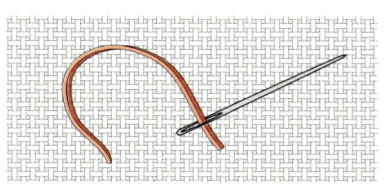

3 Thread two strands of thread into the needle and bring the needle and thread out of the fabric.

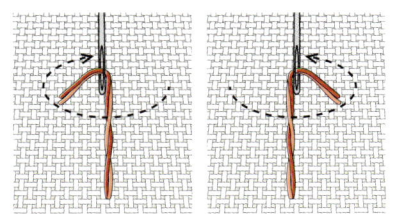

4 Lift up the working thread so that it is perpendicular to the fabric. Twist it either in a clockwise or anticlockwise direction to ensure it is as untwisted as possible.
❶ *This will make the next stitch easier.*

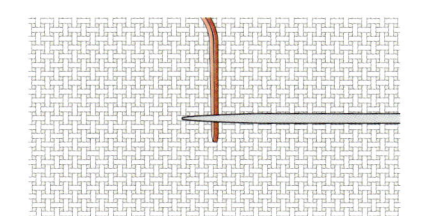

5 Hold the laying tool in your right hand and lay the tip against the untwisted working thread to flatten it upward, back against the fabric.

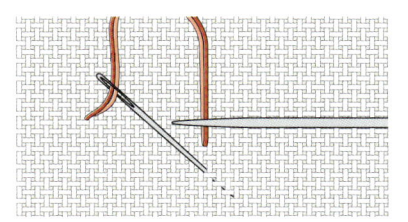

6 Keeping the laying tool in place, insert the needle for the stitch.

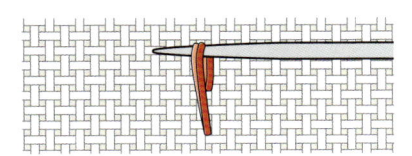

7 Keeping the laying tool in place, pull the needle and thread through until the stitch has no slack between where it enters the fabric and the laying tool.

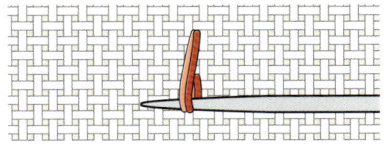

8 Lift the laying tool (keeping the strands untwisted) and gently run it along the inside of the stitch, a little further than the full length of the stitch. Keep tension on the thread as you do this.
❶ *Do not allow the strands to twist.*

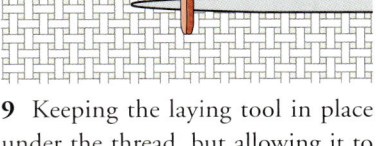

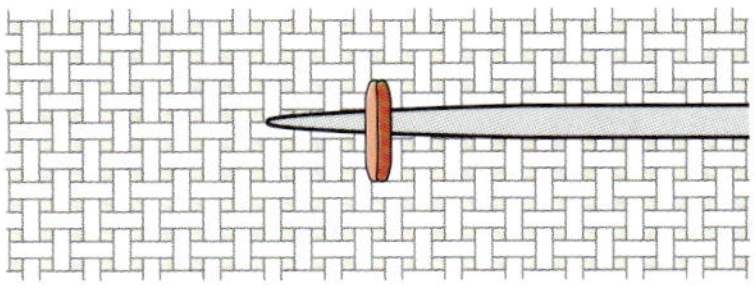

9 Keeping the laying tool in place under the thread, but allowing it to move with the thread, pull the thread through so that the stitch lies flat.
❶ *Keep the strands twist-free between the laying tool and the fabric.*

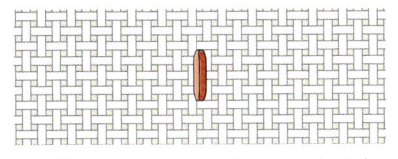

10 Remove the laying tool. The stitch should lie flat with both strands remaining perfectly parallel.

❶ *If the strands twist, insert the laying tool under the stitch. Lift it, sliding/stroking it along the inside of the strands, keeping them twist-free between the laying tool and where they emerged from the fabric. Pull the stitch down into the fabric until there is no twist showing.*

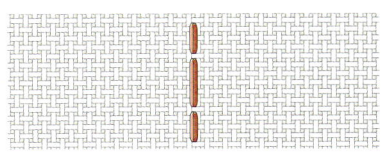

11 Repeat the process for each stitch.
❶ *It may be slow at first, but with practice it will get quicker, and the smooth results will be worth it.*

R using a laying tool

Using a laying tool will help to untwist threads, whether flat silk or multiple thread strands, so that they sit flatter and straighter. By removing the twists, the thread will give better coverage.

A laying tool is a smooth metal, glass or wooden stick with a pointed or rounded end. Tekobaris, trolley needles, stilettos, awls, hatpins, hijab pins, hair sticks, fine double pointed knitting needles and large embroidery needles can all be used as laying tools. Because both hands will be used, mounting the embroidery in a hoop or frame that is on a stand will be advantageous.

A laying tool helps to guide a thread's multiple strands into place so they sit parallel to each other, without twisting (below left, right section) creating a smoother and more uniform finish than twisted threads (below left and right, left sections). When working with flat silk, a laying tool helps the strands to sit wide and flat like a ribbon (below right, right section).

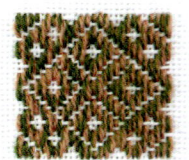

stitching away from yourself with multiple strands

1 Separate all the strands. Bring two of them back together.
❶ *Separating and recombining the strands helps them to intertwine less.*
❶ *These instructions are written for two strands, but more could be used.*

2 Mount the fabric into a hoop or frame so that it is drum tight.
❶ *This allows one hand to be used for the needle, and the other for the laying tool.*

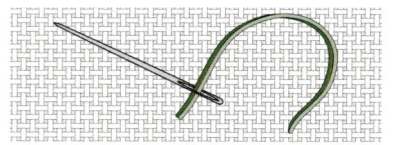

3 Thread two strands of thread into the needle and bring the needle and thread out of the fabric.

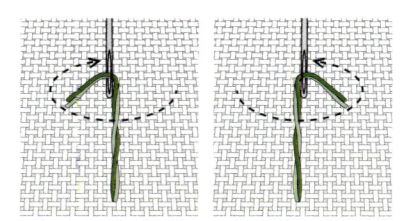

4 Lift up the working thread so that it is perpendicular to the fabric. Twist it either in a clockwise or anticlockwise direction to ensure it is as untwisted as possible.
❶ *This will make the next stitch easier.*

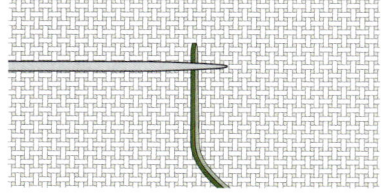

5 Hold the laying tool in your left hand and lay the tip against the untwisted working thread to flatten it downward, back against the fabric.

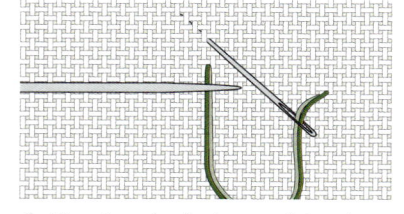

6 Keeping the laying tool in place, insert the needle for the stitch.

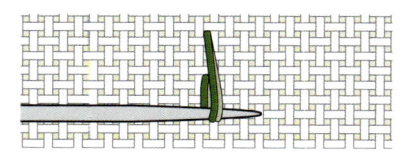

7 Keeping the laying tool in place, pull the needle and thread through until the stitch has no slack between where it enters the fabric and the laying tool.

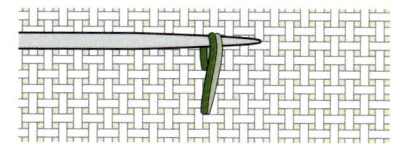

8 Lift the laying tool (keeping the strands untwisted) and gently run it along the inside of the stitch, a little further than the full length of the stitch. Keep tension on the thread as you do this.
❶ *Do not allow the strands to twist.*

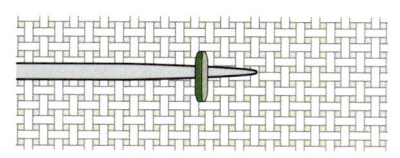

9 Keeping the laying tool in place under the thread, but allowing it to move with the thread, pull the thread through so that the stitch lies flat.
❶ *Keep the strands twist-free between the laying tool and the fabric.*

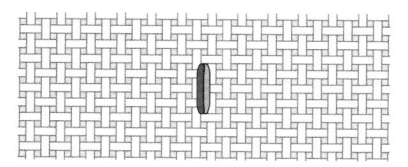

10 Remove the laying tool. The stitch should lie flat with both strands remaining perfectly parallel.

❶ If the strands twist, insert the laying tool under the stitch. Lift it, sliding and stroking it along the inside of the strands, keeping them twist-free between the laying tool and where they emerged from the fabric. Pull the stitch down into the fabric until there is no twist showing.

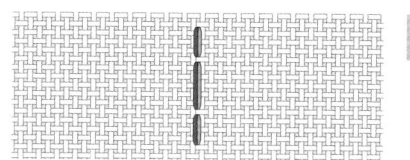

11 Repeat the process for each stitch.
❶ It may be slow at first, but with practice it will get quicker.

stitching toward yourself with multiple strands

1 Separate all the strands. Bring two of them back together.
❶ Separating and recombining the strands helps them to intertwine less.
❶ These instructions are written for two strands, but more could be used.

2 Mount the fabric into a hoop or frame so that it is drum tight.
❶ This allows one hand to be used for the needle, and the other for the laying tool.

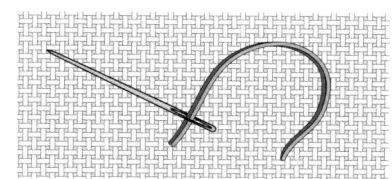

3 Thread two strands of thread into the needle and bring the needle and thread out of the fabric.

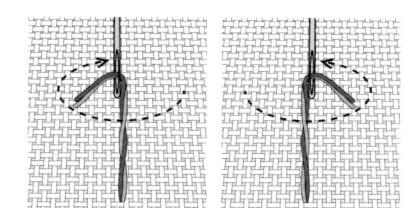

4 Lift up the working thread so that it is perpendicular to the fabric. Twist it either in a clockwise or anticlockwise direction to ensure it is as untwisted as possible.
❶ This will make the next stitch easier.

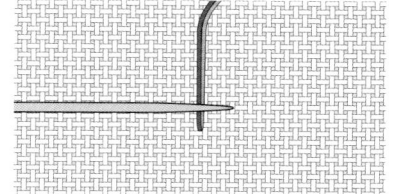

5 Hold the laying tool in your left hand and lay the tip against the untwisted working thread to flatten it upward, back against the fabric.

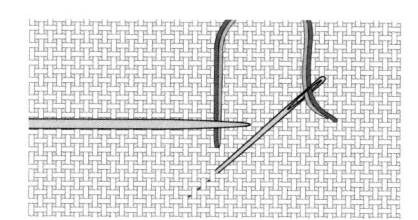

6 Keeping the laying tool in place, insert the needle for the stitch.

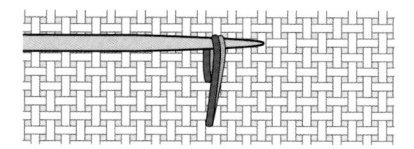

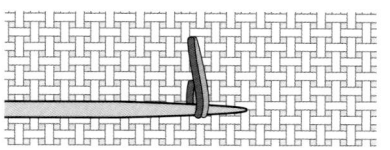

7 Keeping the laying tool in place, pull the needle and thread through until the stitch has no slack between where it enters the fabric and the laying tool.

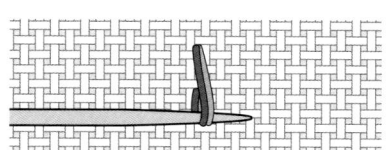

8 Lift the laying tool (keeping the strands untwisted) and gently run it along the inside of the stitch, a little further than the full length of the stitch. Keep tension on the thread as you do this.
❶ Do not allow the strands to twist.

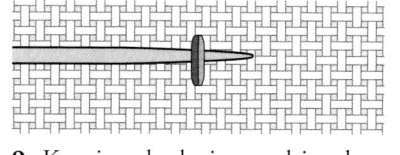

9 Keeping the laying tool in place under the thread, but allowing it to move with the thread, pull the thread through so that the stitch lies flat.
❶ Keep the strands twist-free between the laying tool and the fabric.

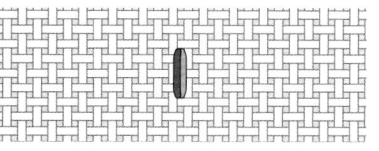

10 Remove the laying tool. The stitch should lie flat with both strands remaining perfectly parallel.

❶ If the strands twist, insert the laying tool under the stitch. Lift it, sliding/stroking it along the inside of the strands, keeping them twist-free between the laying tool and where they emerged from the fabric. Pull the stitch down into the fabric until there is no twist showing.

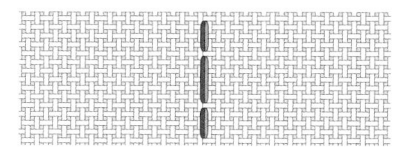

11 Repeat the process for each stitch.
❶ It may be slow at first, but with practice it will get quicker, and the smooth results will be worth it.

satin stitch

Satin stitch is used for diamonds (though sometimes these are also worked in running stitch), åttebladrose petals and the spaces around the petals. Always follow the chart for stitch length and placement. If there is stitching running under the stitching area, use a chenille needle. If not, use a tapestry needle.

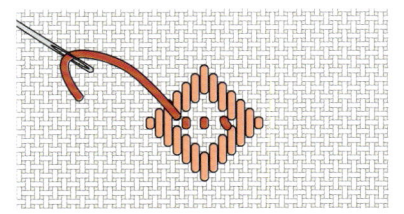

1 Start with a few short stitches under the area to be stitched, similar to the start under top layer running stitching. Bring the needle out at the top of the first stitch to be worked.

❶ *If the base layer of running stitch goes under the space to be satin stitched, use a chenille needle and split the ends of the base layer stitches. If the base layer of stitching does not continue under the space, then use a tapestry needle and stitch as normal with no split stitches.*

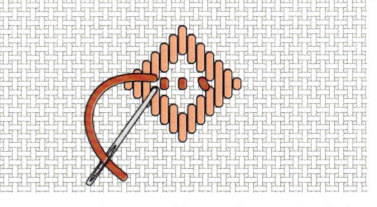

2 Insert the needle at the end of the stitch.

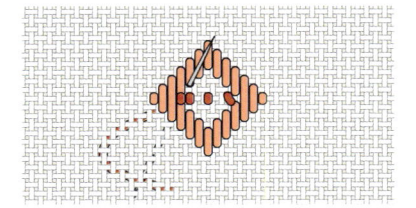

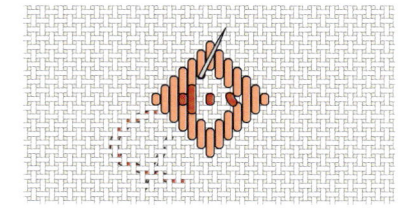

3 Pull the needle through. Bring the needle out at the top of the next stitch across.

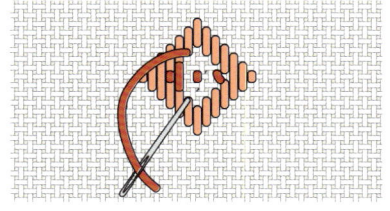

❶ *Satin stitches always start on the same side, unlike running stitches which zig-zag across the space.*

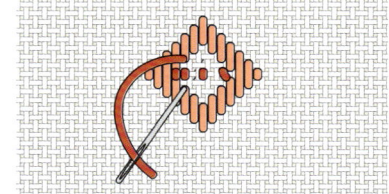

4 Insert the needle at the end of the stitch.

5 Pull the needle through. Bring the needle out at the top of the next stitch across.

6 Insert the needle at the end of the stitch.

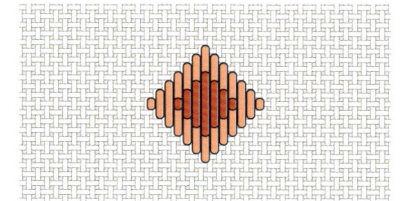

7 Continue in the same manner, coming out at the top, and inserting the needle at the bottom. Complete the shape and finish the thread by running it under the back of the stitches on the back.

88

satin stitch

Satin stitch is used for diamonds (though sometimes these are also worked in running stitch), åttebladrose petals and the spaces around the petals. Always follow the chart for stitch length and placement. If there is stitching running under the stitching area, use a chenille needle. If not, use a tapestry needle.

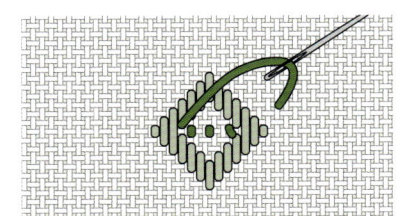

1 Start with a few short stitches under the area to be stitched, similar to the start under top layer running stitching. Bring the needle out at the top of the first stitch to be worked.

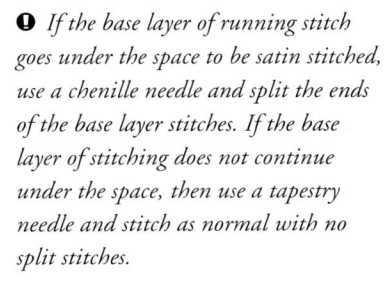

❶ *If the base layer of running stitch goes under the space to be satin stitched, use a chenille needle and split the ends of the base layer stitches. If the base layer of stitching does not continue under the space, then use a tapestry needle and stitch as normal with no split stitches.*

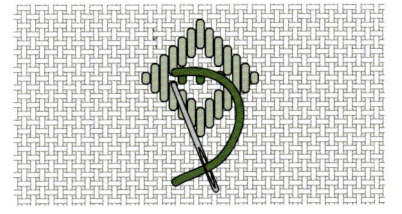

2 Insert the needle at the end of the stitch.

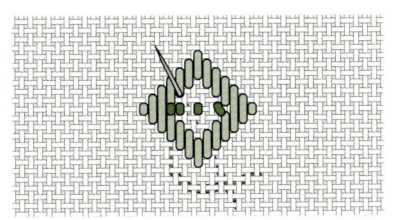

3 Pull the needle through. Bring the needle out at the top of the next stitch across.

❶ *Satin stitches always start on the same side, unlike running stitches which zig-zag across the space.*

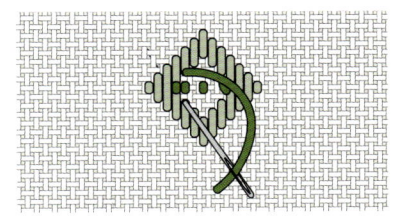

4 Insert the needle at the end of the stitch.

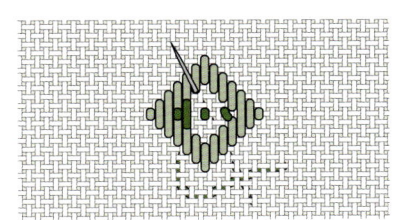

5 Pull the needle through. Bring the needle out at the top of the next stitch across.

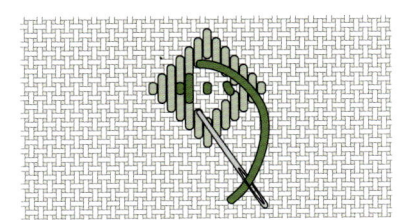

6 Insert the needle at the end of the stitch.

7 Continue in the same manner, coming out at the top, and inserting the needle at the bottom. Complete the shape and finish the thread by running it under the back of the stitches on the back.

stem stitch

Stem stitch can border the top and bottom collar edges. Sometimes it is worked as regular stem stitch on a narrow line, and sometimes it is worked wide, more like a slanting satin stitch. Follow your chart or pattern for stitch length and positioning.

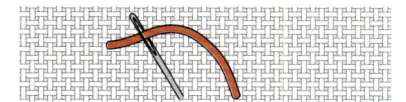

1 Bring the needle out. Insert it six threads to the left.

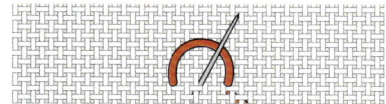

2 Pull the needle through. Leave the stitch curving up. Bring the needle out midway between the stitch ends.
❶ *Not yet tightening the stitch assists with needle placement for the next one.*
❶ *Always bring the needle out below the stitching.*

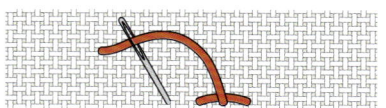

3 Pull the needle through and tighten the thread so the previous stitch lies flat. Insert the needle six threads left of where it emerged, and three from the end of the previous stitch.
❶ *The stitches half overlap each other.*

4 Pull the needle through but leave the stitch curving up gently. Bring the needle out midway along the previous stitch, emerging through the same hole as the end of the first stitch.
❶ *Bring the needle out below the stitch.*

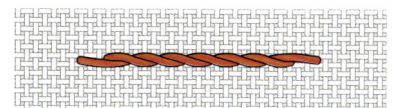

5 Continue in the same way to build up a line of stitching.

wide stem stitch

Wide stem stitch can be worked sloping either left or right. Follow your chart or pattern for stitch length and positioning.

left sloping

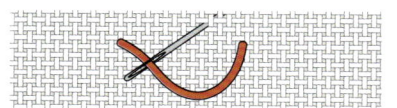

1 Bring the needle out. Insert it four threads to the left and two up.

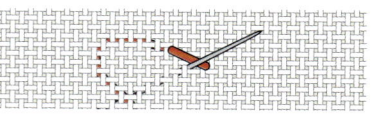

2 Pull the needle through. Bring it out two threads down and right.

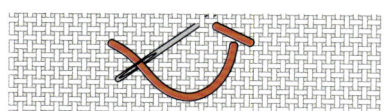

3 Pull the needle through. Insert the needle four threads left and two up.

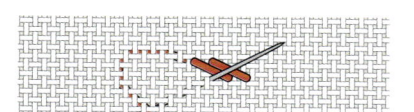

4 Pull the needle through. Bring it out two threads down and right.

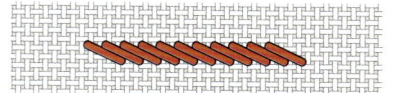

5 Continue in the same way to build up a line of stitching.

right sloping

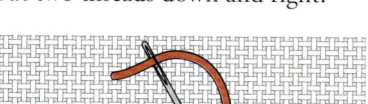

1 Bring the needle out. Insert it four threads to the left and two down.

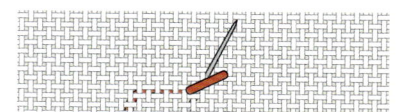

2 Pull the needle through. Bring it out two threads up and right.

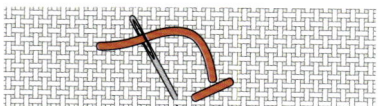

3 Pull the needle through. Insert it four threads left and two down.

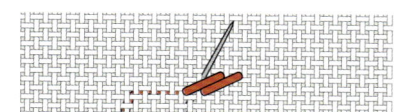

4 Pull the needle through. Bring it out two threads up and right.

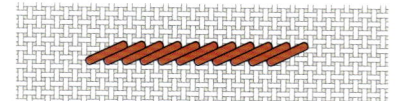

5 Continue in the same way to build up a line of stitching.

stem stitch

TGM-BM.1915:103

Stem stitch can border the top and bottom collar edges. Sometimes it is worked as regular stem stitch on a narrow line, and sometimes it is worked wide, more like a slanting satin stitch. Follow your chart or pattern for stitch length and positioning.

1 Bring the needle out. Insert it six threads to the right.

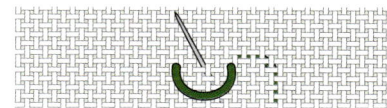

2 Pull the needle through. Leave the stitch hanging down. Bring the needle out midway between the stitch ends.
❶ *Not yet tightening the stitch assists with needle placement for the next one.*
❶ *Always bring the needle out above the stitching.*

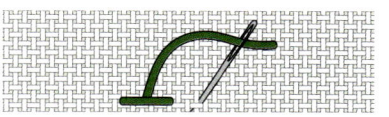

3 Pull the needle through and tighten the thread so the previous stitch lies flat. Insert the needle six threads right of where it emerged, and three from the end of the previous stitch.
❶ *The stitches half overlap each other.*

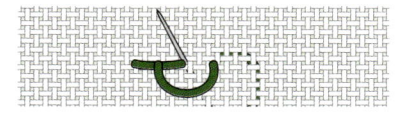

4 Pull the needle through but leave the stitch curving down gently. Bring the needle out midway along the previous stitch, emerging through the same hole as the end of the first stitch.
❶ *Bring the needle out above the stitch.*

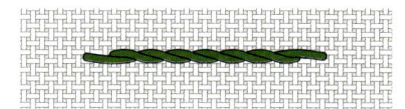

5 Continue in the same way to build up a line of stitching.

wide stem stitch

Wide stem stitch can be worked sloping either left or right. Follow your chart or pattern for stitch length and positioning.

left sloping

TGM-SM.0891

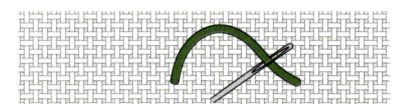

1 Bring the needle out. Insert it four threads to the right and two down.

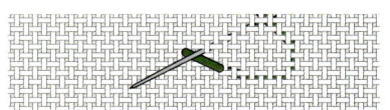

2 Pull the needle through. Bring it out two threads up and to the left.

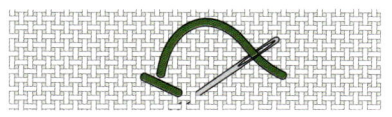

3 Pull the needle through. Insert it four threads right and two down.

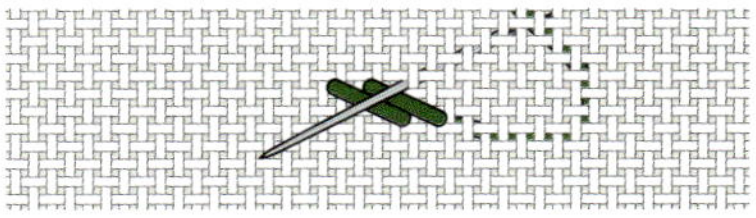

4 Pull the needle through. Bring it out two threads up and to the left.

5 Continue in the same way to build up a line of stitching.

right sloping

TGM-SM.1545

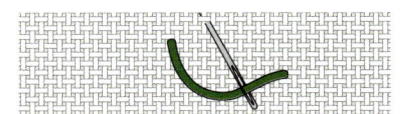

1 Bring the needle out. Insert it four threads to the right and two up.

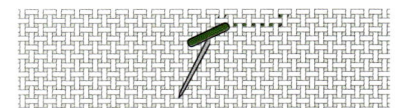

2 Pull the needle through. Bring it out two threads down and left.

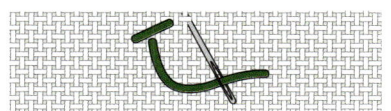

3 Pull the needle through. Insert it four threads right and two up.

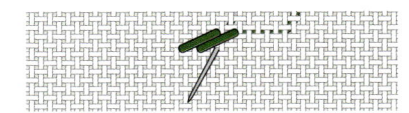

4 Pull the needle through. Bring it out two threads down and left.

5 Continue in the same way to build up a line of stitching.

stitching paths

While there are many different ways a design could be stitched, there are some things to avoid.

As with most styles of embroidery, threads should not be carried a long way. Generally, the longest stitch on the front will span about eight fabric threads. Any more than that, and it becomes unstable.

However, sometimes on the back, you might want to carry your thread further than that. This is particularly relevant when there is a motif of a different colour in the middle of "background" stitching.

On the top band on the band sampler, there is a black motif in the middle of an area of stitching. Should you carry the red across the back to the far side of the space you are leaving for the black, or should you stitch the other side with another thread? It will work better, with less show through, if you work the far side with a separate thread. While it might seem easier to work the red stitching right across from one side of the design to the other, you will get a better result if you do not. This means the design will need to be divided up into sections, to stitch along the design. The two diagrams above show possible options for dividing up the stitching. Some designs just can not be stitched in a neat order, and a lot of stopping and starting will be required.

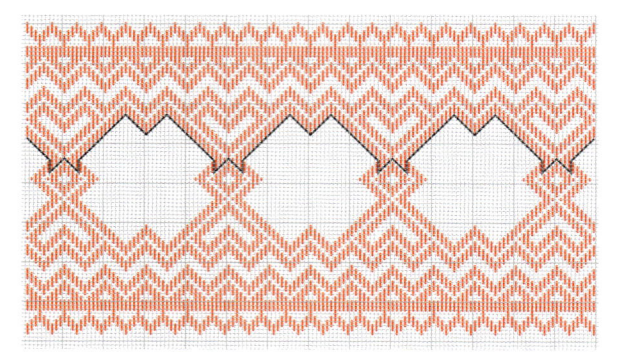

when things go wrong
do not assume

For most designs, it is a matter of counting to three, or one or five for the length of the stitches. However, some designs are more complicated and have stitch lengths of two, four or six etc. Most mistakes come from making assumptions about what is going to happen next with the pattern. Follow the pattern, checking it regularly, and your stitching should be without errors.

too much wear and tear

Do not use thread lengths that are too long. As most stitching for this technique is done with silk or wool, use short lengths rather than long lengths, as both of these fibres will abrade more quickly than linen or cotton. I usually limit my thread length to 50 cm (20 in). Whatever length you use, you will know it is too long if it gets fluffy before you finish using it, or if the wool gets burrs that stop it from going through the fabric evenly.

Use a needle that is large enough for the thread. If it wears too quickly, change to a larger size needle. It might seem too big, but the needle's job is to make a hole large enough for the doubled thread to go through easily. If it doesn't, it will cause wear and tear on the thread.

undoing stitches

When undoing incorrect stitches, there will be less wear and tear on the thread if you unstitch, stitch by stitch, going back into each hole the thread comes out of, rather than pulling the needle off the thread and levering out the stitches.

Unless you have only undone one or two stitches, do not reuse thread that has been undone, as it will more readily show signs of wear and tear on reuse, such as being fluffier or thinner than normal.

Particularly when wool threads have been removed, they can leave fibres in the fabric. A "boo boo stick", which is a small round brush with spiky bristles (shown below), can help to remove these remaining fibres. Otherwise, carefully pick them out with your fingers.

withdrawing threads

Threads need to be withdrawn to create the tooth edging. Withdraw six threads for short teeth; use eight or more for longer teeth. When threads are withdrawn for projects in this book, they can be withdrawn across the entire width of the fabric. Finer counts of fabric can often benefit from more threads being removed, rather than fewer.

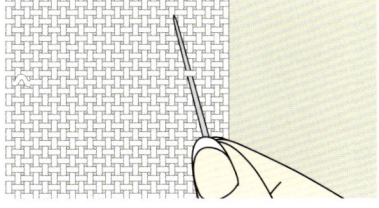

1 Slide the point of a tapestry needle under the first thread to be withdrawn, a few threads away from the fabric edge.

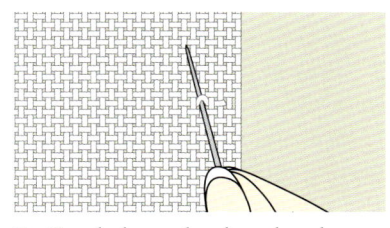

2 Gently lever the thread end up…

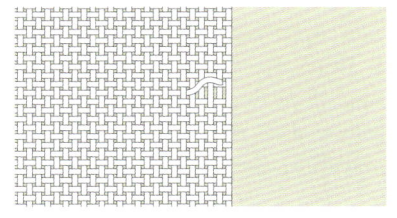

3 …and out of the fabric.

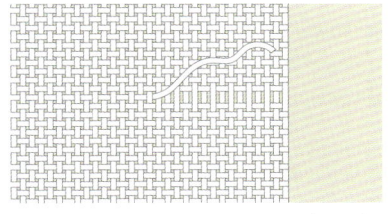

4 Moving along about ten threads, lever the thread end up and out of the fabric again.

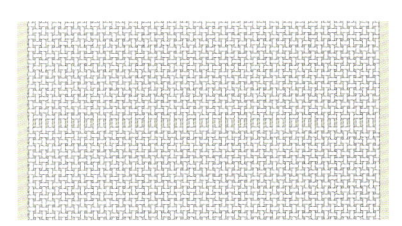

5 Continue, moving along about ten threads each time, levering the thread out of the fabric, until the whole thread is withdrawn.
❶ *Do not lever the thread up in between every vertical thread. There is no advantage in this and it makes the process much slower.*

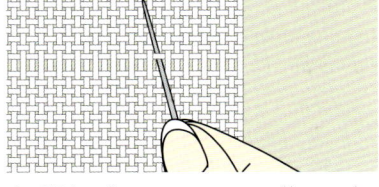

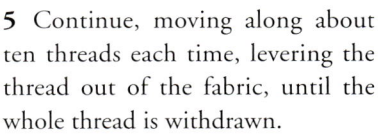

6 Slide the tapestry needle under the next thread to be removed, near the edge of the fabric.

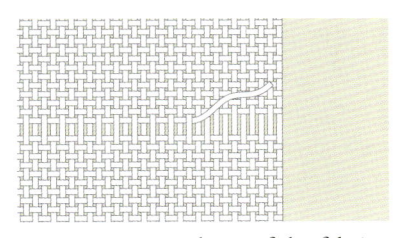

7 Lever it up and out of the fabric.
❶ *It will be much easier this time seeing a thread has already been withdrawn.*

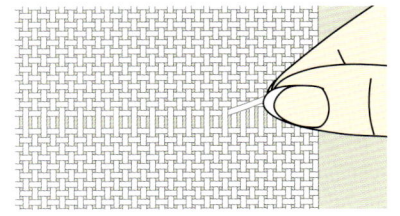

8 Grab hold of the thread end and pull it out through the fabric.
❶ *Use tweezers if they provide better grip strength for you.*

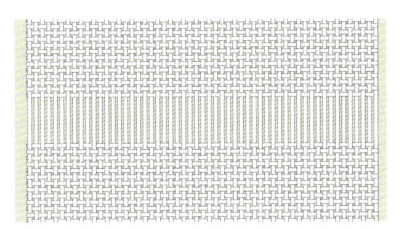

9 Withdraw as many threads as are required by the pattern.
❶ *Between six and ten threads would be usual.*

tooth edging

This collar edging is known as mouse tags in Norway. Threads are usually woven in groups of three (as shown) for Telemark collars, and in multiples of four for those from Hardanger. Do not use a hoop.

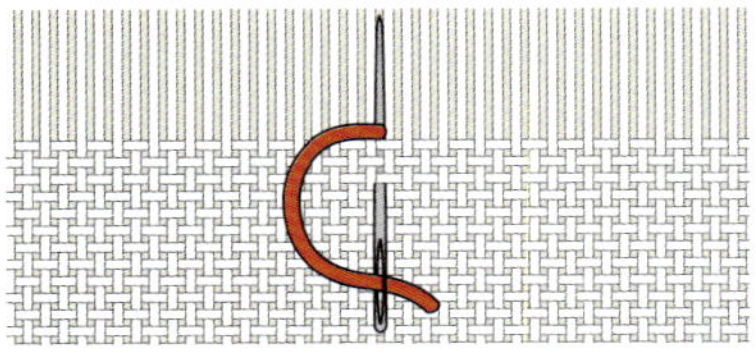

1 Bring the needle out at the lower edge of the drawn thread area. From below, slide the needle under the next three threads down.

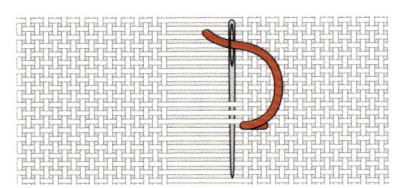

2 Turn the work 90 degrees anti-clockwise. Pull the needle through. From above, slide the needle under the next three threads up.

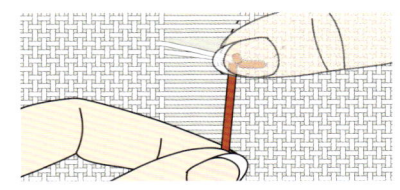

3 Pinch the stitch between your finger and thumb. With the other hand, pull the thread to tighten the stitch.
❶ *Do this after each stitch.*

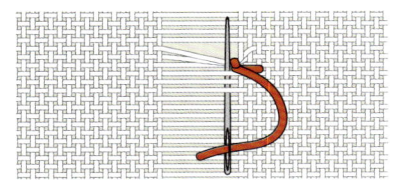

4 Moving left, from below, slide the needle under the next three threads down from where the thread emerges.

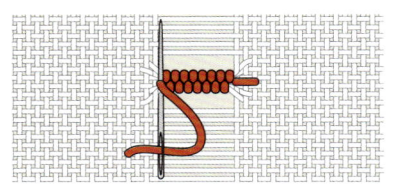

5 Pinch and pull to tighten. Continue weaving until the bar is full, finishing with a stitch on the lower group.

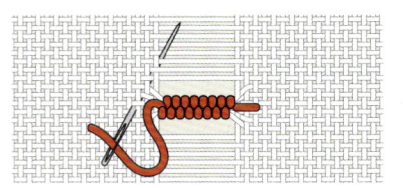

6 Insert the needle three threads to the left. Bring it out six threads up and three right, midway up the next bar.

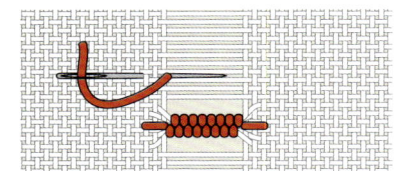

7 Pull the needle through. Take the needle under the three threads to the left of where the thread emerged.

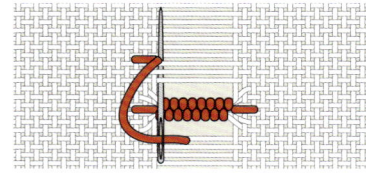

8 Pull the needle through. Moving right, from below, slide the needle under the third group of three threads.

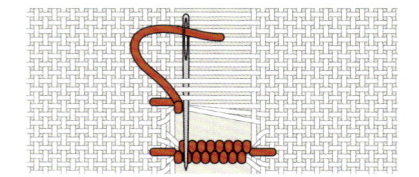

9 Moving right, from above, slide the needle under the fourth group of three threads.

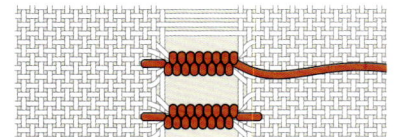

10 Fill the bar, finishing with a stitch on the upper group.
❶ *Each bar should have the same number of stitches.*

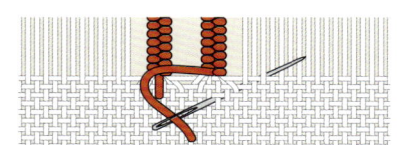

11 Turn the work 90 degrees clockwise. Insert the needle three threads down. Bring it out six threads right and three up.

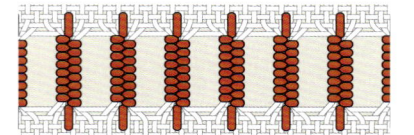

12 Continue weaving bars, cycling through Steps 1 to 11.

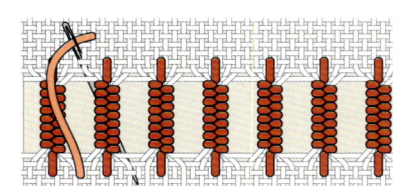

13 Bring a thread out between the first two bars, three threads away from the weaving area. Insert the needle three threads away on the far side. Bring it out three threads out, between the next bars on the first side.

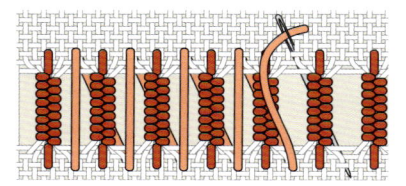

14 Work a few more stitches in a similar manner, taking a stitch between each of the bars.

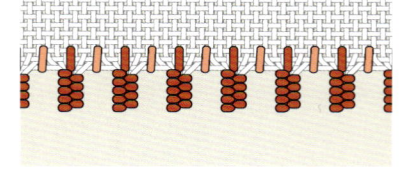

15 Pull the thread to draw the sides together tightly, folding each woven bar. Continue, stitching between a few bars, then drawing them tightly together, across the entire width.

kvalesaum

This stitching is worked in conjunction with the tooth edging. The second row of stitching is often worked in a different colour of thread. Work with the tooth edging at the bottom. When the teeth are worked over groups of four threads, use multiples of four threads for the kvalesaum also. Do not use a hoop of frame.

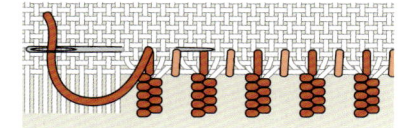

1 Bring the needle out three threads up from the middle of the first woven bar. Insert the needle three threads to the left, and bring it out six threads to the right.

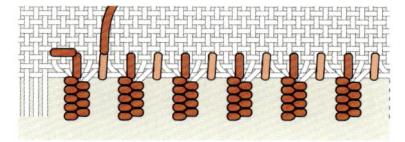

2 Pull the needle and thread through so that the stitch sits gently on the fabric surface.
- *This stitching is usually only stitched through the front layer of fabric.*

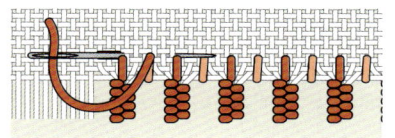

3 Insert the needle three threads to the left, at the end of the previous stitch, and bring it out six threads to the right.
- *This row is a row of backstitch.*

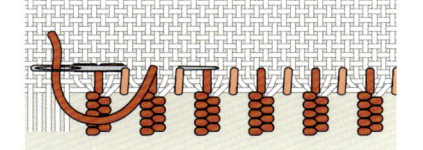

4 Pull the needle and thread through so that the stitch sits gently on the fabric surface. Insert the needle three threads to the left, at the end of the previous stitch, and bring it out six threads to the right.

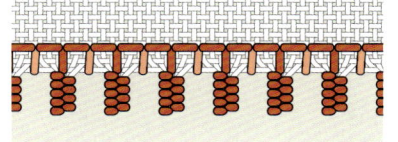

5 Continue in the same manner to build up a line of stitching that is the same length as the tooth edging.
- *For smøyg collars from Hardanger, cease stitching the kvalesaum here, with just the line of backstitch.*

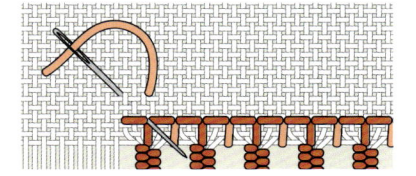

6 Continuing with the same colour, or switching to a new colour, bring the needle out three threads up from the previous line, and three threads in from the end. Insert the needle three threads to the left and bring it out three threads down and right.
- *Work through both fabric layers.*

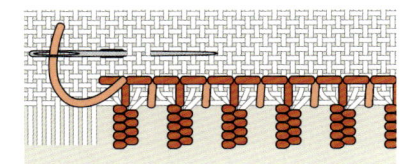

7 Pull the needle and thread through so that the stitch sits gently on the fabric surface. Insert the needle three threads up and bring it out three threads to the right.

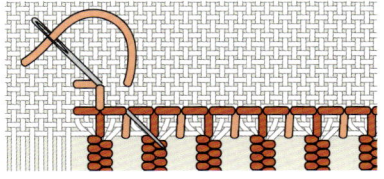

8 Pull the needle and thread through so that the stitch sits gently on the fabric surface. Insert the needle three threads to the left and bring it out three threads down and right.

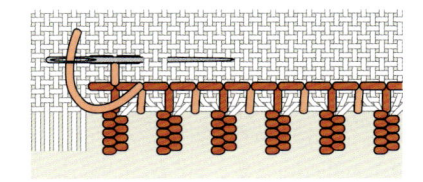

9 Pull the needle and thread through so that the stitch sits gently on the fabric surface. Insert the needle three threads up and bring it out three threads to the right.

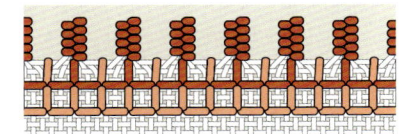

10 Continue in the same way to build up a line of stitching. Turn the work 180 degrees to see it the right way up.

tooth edging

This collar edging is known as mouse tags in Norway. Threads are usually woven in groups of three (as shown) for Telemark collars, and in multiples of four for those from Hardanger. Do not use a hoop.

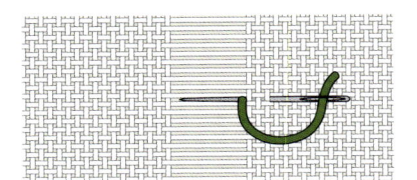

1 Bring the needle out at the right edge of the drawn thread area. Insert the needle three threads to the right and bring it out three to the left.

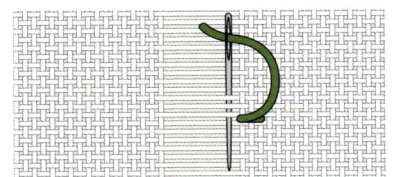

2 Pull the needle through. From above, slide the needle under the next three threads up.

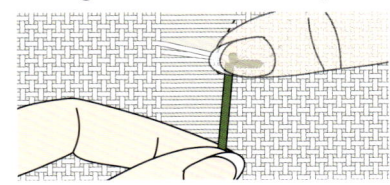

3 Pinch the stitch between your finger and thumb. With the other hand, pull the thread to tighten the stitch.
❶ *Do this after each stitch.*

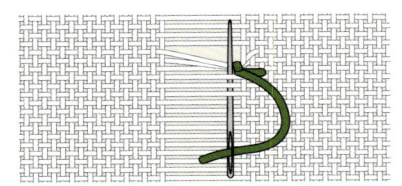

4 Moving left, from below, slide the needle under the next three threads down from where the thread emerges.

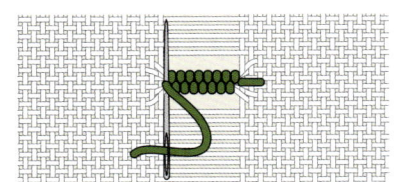

5 Pinch and pull to tighten. Continue weaving until the bar is full, finishing with a stitch on the lower group.

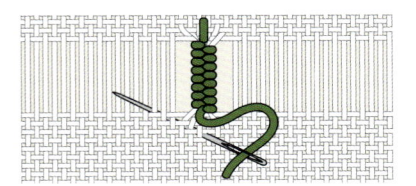

6 Turn the work 90 degrees anticlockwise. Insert the needle three threads down. Bring it out six threads left and three up.

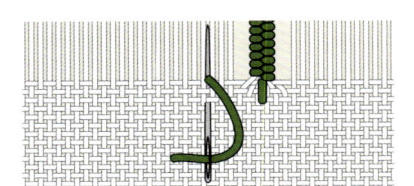

7 Pull the needle through. Insert the needle three threads down and bring it out three up.

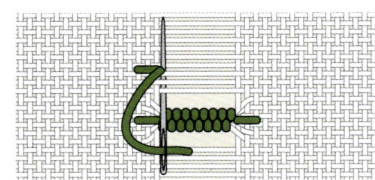

8 Turn the work back. Pull the needle through. From below, slide the needle under the third group of three threads.

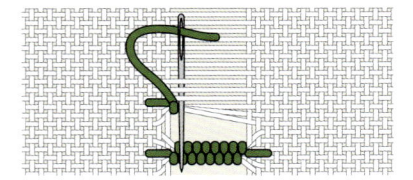

9 Moving right, from above, slide the needle under the fourth group of three threads.

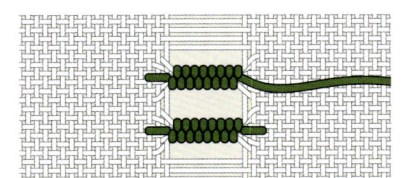

10 Fill the bar, finishing with a stitch on the upper group.
❶ *All bars need the same stitch quantity.*

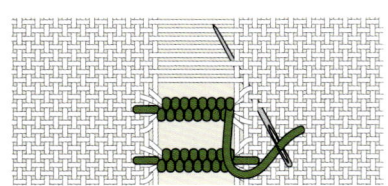

11 Insert the needle three threads right. Bring it out six threads up and three left.

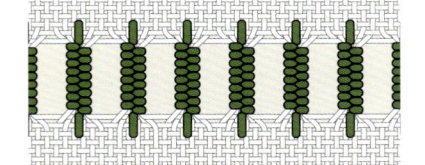

12 Continue weaving bars, cycling through Steps 1 to 11.

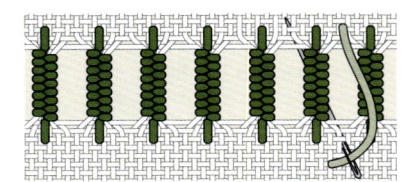

13 Bring a thread out between the first two bars, three threads away from the weaving area. Insert the needle three threads away on the far side. Bring it out three threads out, between the next bars on the first side.

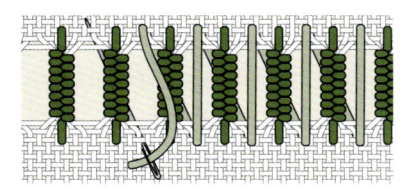

14 Work a few more stitches in a similar manner, taking a stitch between each of the bars.

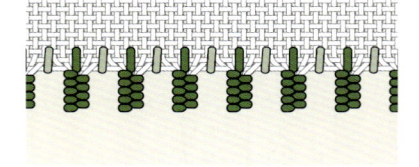

15 Pull the thread to draw the sides together tightly, folding each woven bar. Continue, stitching between a few bars, then drawing them tightly together, across the entire width.

kvalesaum

This stitching is worked in conjunction with the tooth edging. The second row of stitching is often worked in a different colour of thread. Work with the tooth edging at the bottom. When the teeth are worked over groups of four threads, use multiples of four threads for the kvalesaum also. Do not use a hoop or frame.

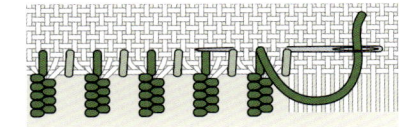

1 Bring the needle out three threads up from the middle of the first woven bar. Insert the needle three threads to the right, and bring it out six threads to the left.

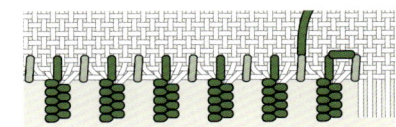

2 Pull the needle and thread through so that the stitch sits gently on the fabric surface.
❶ *This stitching is usually only stitched through the front layer of fabric.*

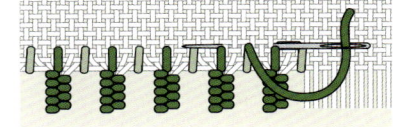

3 Insert the needle three threads to the right, at the end of the previous stitch, and bring it out six threads to the left.
❶ *This row is a row of backstitch.*

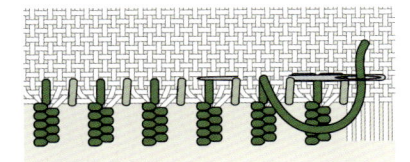

4 Pull the needle and thread through so that the stitch sits gently on the fabric surface. Insert the needle three threads to the right, at the end of the previous stitch, and bring it out six threads to the left.

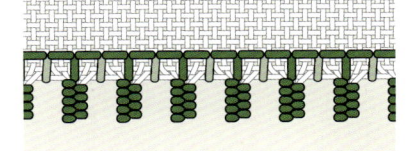

5 Continue in the same manner to build up a line of stitching that is the same length as the tooth edging.
❶ *For smøyg collars from Hardanger, cease stitching the kvalesaum here, with just the line of backstitch.*

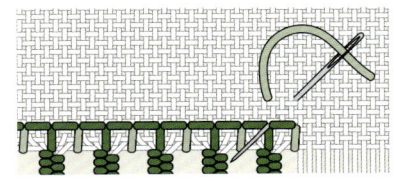

6 Continuing with the same colour, or switching to a new colour, bring the needle out three threads up from the previous line, and three threads in from the end. Insert the needle three threads to the right and bring it out three threads down and left.
❶ *Work through both fabric layers.*

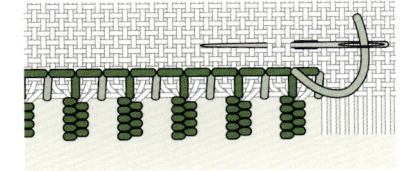

7 Pull the needle and thread through so that the stitch sits gently on the fabric surface. Insert the needle three threads up and bring it out three threads to the left.

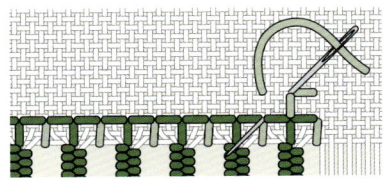

8 Pull the needle and thread through so that the stitch sits gently on the fabric surface. Insert the needle three threads to the right and bring it out three threads down and left.

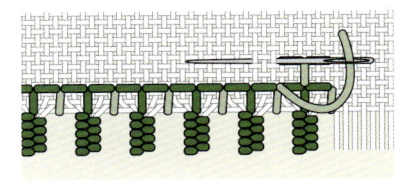

9 Pull the needle and thread through so that the stitch sits gently on the fabric surface. Insert the needle three threads up and bring it out three threads to the left.

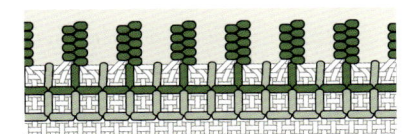

10 Continue in the same way to build up a line of stitching. Turn the work 180 degrees to see it the right way up.

lacing fabric

This technique can be used to tightly stretch embroidered or plain fabric over a board, to prepare them for finishing. The board can be padded or unpadded.

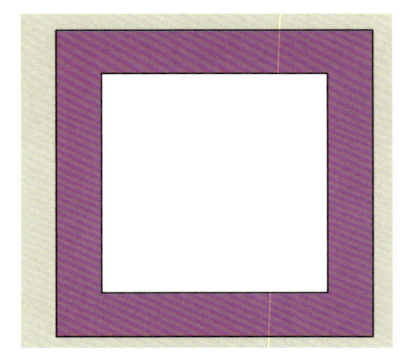

1 Centre the cardboard over the back of the fabric.
❶ *If there is embroidery on the fabric, make sure it is exactly centred.*

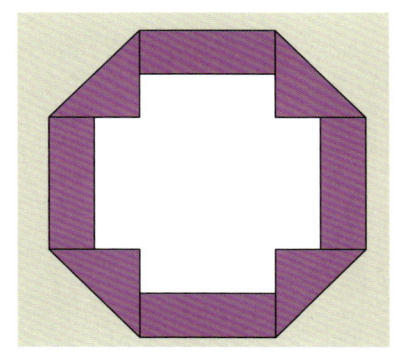

2 Fold the corners of the fabric in over the corners of the cardboard. Finger press.
❶ *Folding in the corners will help to reduce bulk, and give a neater corner.*

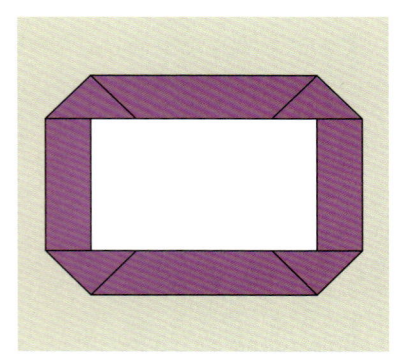

3 Keeping the corners in place, fold down the top and bottom sides.

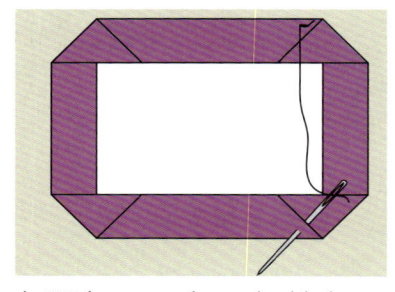

4 With a very long doubled-over thread, start in the top right corner with a few backstitches. Take the needle across to the other side and bring it out through the folded flap.

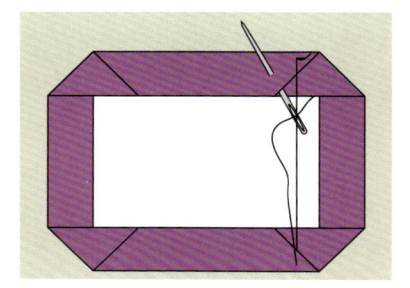

5 Pull the needle and thread through and tighten. Take the needle across to the other side and bring it out through the folded flap.
❶ *The idea is that the thread is very tight, so that the fabric is stretched taut around the board.*

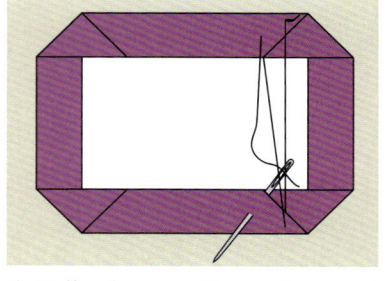

6 Pull the needle and thread through and tighten. Take the needle across to the other side and bring it out through the folded flap.

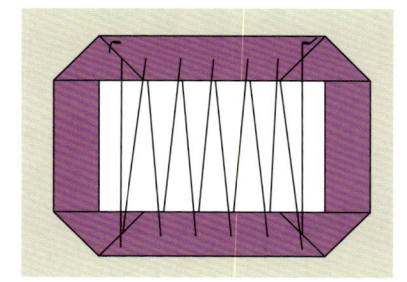

7 Keep working back and forth between the folded flaps. Ensure that the thread is very taut before ending off with a few back stitches.
❶ *Before finishing, return to the beginning of the lacing, and tighten each thread in succession, taking out any slack.*

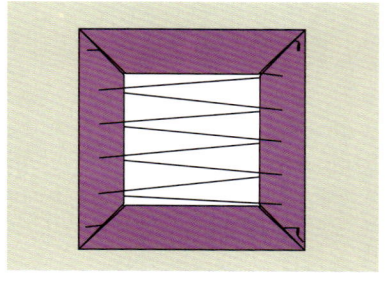

8 Turn the work 90 degrees and fold in the other flaps.
❶ *If you are lacing an embroidery, before this step, turn the work over and check that it is centred. Make any necessary adjustments before continuing.*

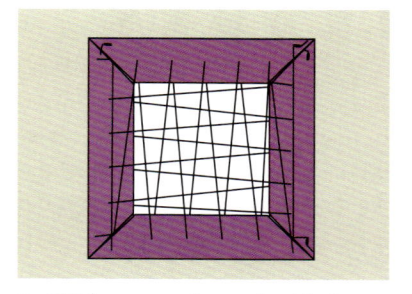

9 With a new long doubled-over thread, lace the second set of flaps tightly.

folding the hem and mitring the corners

1 With the wrong side of the fabric face up, on one side, fold in the first fold for the hem. Finger press to make a crease.

2 Fold the same amount in again, to encase the raw edge. Press.

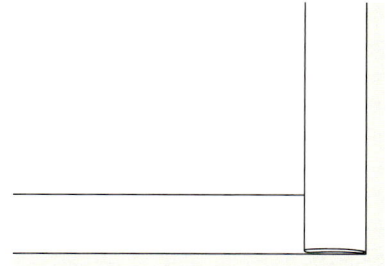

3 On the adjacent side, using the same measurements as for the first side, fold in twice, and press.

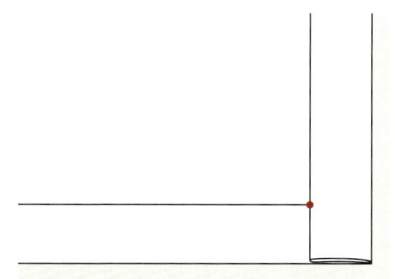

4 Where the two folds meet, mark with a wash-out pencil or HB pencil.

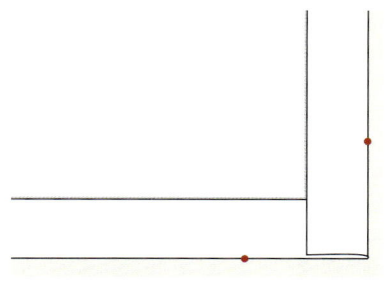

5 Unfold the second fold on each side.

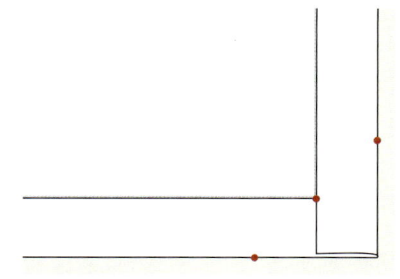

6 Where the two remaining folds meet, mark again.

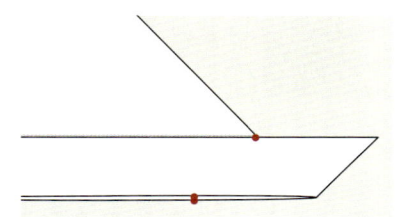

7 With the hems on the outside, fold the fabric diagonally through the corner, matching the dots on the edges of the fabric. Let the extra fabric at the corner unfold.

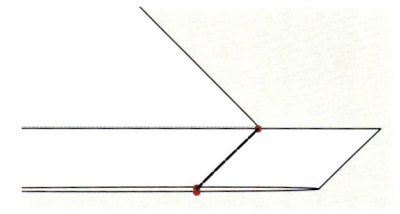

8 Mark a line between the two dots. This is the stitching line. Sew along the line, keeping the first hem folds in place.

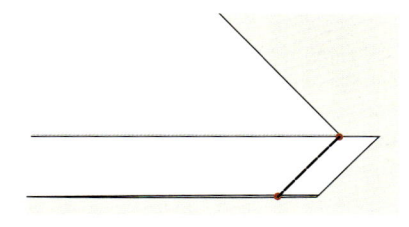

9 Trim the mitre seam allowance to 6 mm (¼ in).

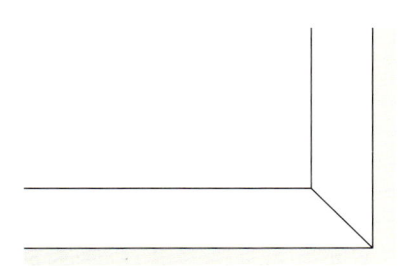

❶ *Once the hem corner has been mitred, you can then either sew the hem by hand or machine.*

10 Turn the corner the right way out, with the seam open flat and the first hem fold tucked inside the hem.

appendix: fabric and thread compatibility

Not all threads are available in all markets. This appendix shows samples of threads stitched on different counts of fabric, to help you assess which ones give the coverage you need. Keep in mind that some thread ranges have a limited spread of colours, so if you're substituting a thread, the appropriate colour may not exist in your chosen range.

When stitching smøyg, you want good coverage of the ground fabric. You don't want obvious white showing between threads. These samples (shown actual size) are worked in black because black has the most contrast with the white fabric. If the white fabric is going to show up between any coloured stitches, it will show up most between the black ones because that has the most contrast. So if the coverage is good in a particular thread in black, it will work fine for other colours too.

A lighter colour will often appear to have better coverage than black would, even if the thread is the same thickness, because the contrast is less pronounced.

Suggested needle sizes are given, which apply to both tapestry and chenille needles.

50 count fabric (20 threads per cm)

All threads use a single strand.

Anchor Silk. *100% silk. Needle: 26 Coverage: Good*

Aurifil Lana. *50% wool, 50% acrylic. Needle: 24 Coverage: Thick*

Au Ver à Soie 1003. *100% silk. Needle: 26 Coverage: Thin*

Au Ver à Soie Soie Gobelins. *100% silk. Needle: 26 Coverage: Thin*

Au Ver à Soie Soie d'Alger. *100% silk. Needle: 26 Coverage: Good*

Classic Colorworks Belle Soie. *100% silk. Needle: 26 Coverage: Good*

Devere Yarns Worsted Wool. *100% wool. Needle: 24 Coverage: Good*

The Gentle Art Simply Wool. *100% Wool. Needle: 24 Coverage: Thick*

Gloriana 12 strand silk. *100% silk. Needle: 26 Coverage: Good*

Gloriana Luminescence. *100% silk. Needle: 26 Coverage: Thin*

Gloriana Lorikeet. *100% wool. Needle: 24 Coverage: Good*

Gütermann R753. *100% silk. Needle: 26 Coverage: Good*

Gütermann S303. *100% silk. Needle: 26 Coverage: Thin*

Madeira Silk. *100% silk. Needle: 26 Coverage: Good*

Needlepoint Inc Silk. *100% silk. Needle: 26 Coverage: Good*

Rainbow Gallery Splendor. *100% silk. Needle: 26 Coverage: Good*

Ets Toulemonde Laine Saint Pierre *50% wool, 50% polyamide. Needle: 24 Coverage: Good*

Tire Hand Sewing Thread No 9. *100% silk. Needle: 26 Coverage: Thin*

Venne Organic Merino Wool Nm 28/2. *100% wool. Needle: 24 Coverage: Thick*

Vineyard Merino Strandable. *100% wool. Needle: 26 Coverage: Good*

Wonderfil Ellana. *50% wool, 50% acrylic. Needle: 24 Coverage: Thick*

100

40 count fabric (16 threads per cm)

All threads use a single strand.

Aurifil Lana. *50% wool, 50% acrylic. Needle: 24* Coverage: Good

Au Ver à Soie Fine d'Aubusson wool. *100% wool. Needle: 24* Coverage: Good

Au Ver à Soie Soie d'Alger. *100% silk. Needle: 26* Coverage: Thin

Au Ver à Soie Soie Ovale. *100% silk. Needle: 24 and laying tool* Coverage: Thick

Au Ver à Soie Soie Perlée. *100% silk. Needle: 26* Coverage: Good

Bella Lusso Wool. *100% wool. Needle: 24* Coverage: Good

Devere Yarns No 36 silk. *100% silk. Needle: 24* Coverage: Good

Devere Yarns Worsted Wool. *100% wool. Needle: 24* Coverage: Thin

Fru Zippe Flora wool. *100% wool. Needle: 24* Coverage: Good

The Gentle Art Simply Wool. *100% Wool. Needle: 24* Coverage: Good

Gloriana Lorikeet. *100% wool. Needle: 24* Coverage: Good

Gloriana Princess Perle Petite Silk. *100% silk. Needle: 24* Coverage: Good

Gumnut Yarns Daisies. *100% wool. Needle: 24* Coverage: Good

Gütermann R753. *100% silk. Needle: 26* Coverage: Good

Madeira Silk. *100% silk. Needle: 26* Coverage: Thin

Borgs Mora Wool. *100% wool. Needle: 24* Coverage: Good

Rainbow Gallery Splendor. *100% silk. Needle: 26* Coverage: Good

Rainbow Gallery Wisper. *70% kid mohair, 30% nylon. Needle: 22* Coverage: Thick

Rustic Wool Moire. *100% wool. Needle: 22* Coverage: Thick

Tapisserie de France Wool. *100% wool. Needle: 24* Coverage: Good

Tire Button Hole Thread No 16. *100% silk. Needle: 24* Coverage: Good

Venne Organic Merino Wool Nm 28/2. *100% wool. Needle: 24* Coverage: Good

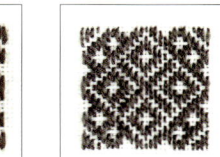

Vineyard Merino Strandable. *100% wool. Needle: 26* Coverage: Thin

Wonderfil Ellana. *50% wool, 50% acrylic. Needle: 24* Coverage: Good

101

34 count fabric (13 threads per cm)

All threads use a single strand.

Au Ver à Soie Fine d'Aubusson wool. *100% wool. Needle: 24* Coverage: Good

Au Ver à Soie Soie Ovale. *100% silk. Needle: 24 and laying tool* Coverage: Good

Au ver a Soie Soie Perlée. *100% silk. Needle: 26* Coverage: Thin

Bella Lusso Wool. *100% wool. Needle: 24* Coverage: Good

Devere Yarns No 36 silk. *100% silk. Needle: 24* Coverage: Good

Fru Zippe Flora wool. *100% wool. Needle: 24* Coverage: Thin

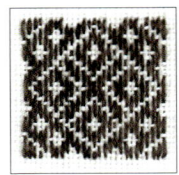

Gloriana Lorikeet. *100% wool. Needle: 24* Coverage: Good

Gumnut Yarns Daisies. *100% wool. Needle: 24* Coverage: Good

Borgs Mora Wool. *100% wool. Needle: 24* Coverage: Good

Rainbow Gallery Elegance. *100% silk. Needle: 22* Coverage: Good

Renaissance Dyeing Crewel Wool. *100% lambswool. Needle: 24* Coverage: Good

Rustic Wool Moire. *100% wool. Needle: 22* Coverage: Thick

Tapisserie de France Wool. *100% wool. Needle: 24* Coverage: Thin

Tire Button Hole Thread No 16. *100% silk. Needle: 24* Coverage: Thin

Venne Organic Merino Wool Nm 28/2. *100% wool. Needle: 24* Coverage: Good

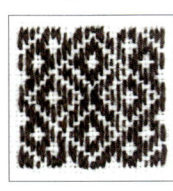

Wonderfil Ellana. *50% wool, 50% acrylic. Needle: 24* Coverage: Thin

28 count fabric (11 threads per cm)

Some threads use a single strand; some use two.

Appletons Crewel Wool. *100% Wool. Needle: 22* Coverage: Good

Au Ver à Soie Soie Ovale. *100% silk. Needle: 24 and laying tool* Coverage: Good

Bella Lusso Wool. *100% wool. Needle: 24* Coverage: Thin

Cottage Garden Threads 2 ply merino wool. *100% wool. Needle: 22* Coverage: Thick

Gloriana Lorikeet – 2 strands. *100% wool. Needle: 22 and laying tool* Coverage: Good

Gumnut Yarns Blossoms. *100% wool. Needle: 22* Coverage: Good

Rainbow Gallery Elegance. *100% silk. Needle: 22* Coverage: Good

Renaissance Dyeing Crewel Wool. *100% lambswool. Needle: 24* Coverage: Good

Rustic Wool Moire. *100% wool. Needle: 22.* Coverage: Good

Vineyard Merino Strandable – 2 strands. *100% wool. Needle: 22 and laying tool* Coverage: Good

image credits

All photographs not listed below are © Copyright Yvette Stanton 2018. Other images are as listed. Every effort has been made to trace the copyright holders and obtain permission to reproduce images. The publisher apologises for any errors or omissions in this list.

The following shorthand is used:
YS: Yvette Stanton,
NFM: Norsk Folkemuseum
HVM: Hardanger og Voss Museum
TM: Telemark Museum
VTM: Vest-Telemark Museum

Listings go clockwise, starting top left and spiralling inward on the page.

P5: © YS; NF.1911-1264 © Haakon Michael Harriss / NFM, used under CC BY-SA. Source: digitaltmuseum.org; NF.1921-0661 © YS, permission of NFM; VF.09374 © Caroline Omlid / Slottsfjellsmuseet, used under CC BY-SA. Source: digitaltmuseum.org

P6: © YS; © YS; NF.1955-0441 © NFM, used under CC BY-SA. Source: digitaltmuseum.org; HFU-17926 © YS, permission of HVM; NF2000-1699 © YS, permission of NFM; Brudedrakter fra Hardanger, Image number: blds_04024 © Normanns kunstforlag A/S, used by permission, Nasjonalbiblioteket / National Library of Norway; NF.1921-0661 © YS, permission of NFM; NF1899-0171 © YS, permission of NFM; NF.2001-0211 © NFM, used under CC BY-SA. Source: digitaltmuseum.org; FYB.00099 © VTM, used under CC BY-SA. Source: digitaltmuseum.org; NF.1911-0997 © Anne-Lise Reinsfelt / NFM, used under CC BY-SA. Source: digitaltmuseum.org; © YS, permission of HVM.

P7: Kogin embroidery © YS, permission of Amuse Museum, Tokyo, Japan; Danish darning sampler © YS, collection of Aafke Buurs, used by permission; 83.603 © The Walters Art Museum; used under CC0.

P8: NF.2000-0162 © YS, permission of NFM; NF.1899-0171 © YS, permission of NFM; TGM-SM.2576 © YS, permission of TM; NF.1949-0545 © Haakon Michael Harriss / NFM, used under CC BY-SA. Source: digitaltmuseum.org.

P9: TGM-SM.2813 © YS, permission of TM; TGM-SM.0710 © YS, permission of TM; TGM-SM.3418 © YS, permission of TM; TGM-BM.1915:093 © YS, permission of TM; TGM-SM.0712 © YS, permission of TM; TGM-BM.1913:411 © YS, permission of TM; TGM-SM.1288 © YS, permission of TM; NF.1896-0692 © YS, permission of TM.

P10: NF.2000-0612 © YS, permission of NFM; NF.2000-0612 © YS, permission of NFM; TGM-SM.0629, TGM-SM.0626, TGM-SM.0719, TGM-SM.0893, TGM-BM.1941-42:091 © YS, permission of TM; VF.09376 © Caroline Omlid / Slottsfjellsmuseet, used under CC BY-SA. Source: digitaltmuseum.org; TGM-BM.1987:374 © YS, permission of TM; NF.2000-0612 © YS, permission of NFM.

P11: NF.2000-0162 © YS, permission of NFM; HFU.18293 © YS, permission of HVM; HFU.18363 © YS, permission of HVM; HFU.2485 © YS, permission of HVM; HFU.3119 © YS, permission of HVM; NF.1955-0457 © YS, permission of NFM; NF.1955-0305C © YS, permission of NFM.

P12: NF.1911-0008 © YS, permission of NFM; HFU.10648 © YS, permission of NFM; HFU.10648 © YS, permission of NFM; HFU.347 © YS, permission of NFM; © YS, permission of HVM; Bondebryllup i Hardanger, © Finn Norstrøm, used by permission, Riksarkivet (National Archives of Norway); NF.1911-0008 © YS, permission of NFM.

P13: © YS, permission of HVM; NF.2000-1699 © YS, permission of NFM; BUM.2047 © YS, permission of HVM; BUM.2055 © YS, permission of HVM; HFU.18370 © YS, permission of HVM; HFU.1177 © YS, permission of HVM; HFU.675 © YS, permission of HVM; HFU.18368 © YS, permission of HVM; BUM.2059 © YS, permission of HVM; HFU.352 © YS, permission of HVM; HFU.177 © YS, permission of HVM; HFU.2385 © YS, permission of HVM; HFU.18463 © YS, permission of HVM.

P14: NF.2001-0067A © YS, permission of NFM; NF.2001-0240 © NFM, used under CC BY-SA. Source: digitaltmuseum.org; NF.2001-0240 © Anne-Lise Reinsfelt / NFM, used under CC BY-SA. Source: digitaltmuseum.org; NF.2001-0067A © YS, permission of NFM.

P15: NF.1921-0661 © YS, permission of NFM; © YS, permission of HVM; NF.1992-2424 © YS, permission of NFM; NF.1955-0441 © NFM, used under CC BY-SA. Source: digitaltmuseum.org.

P16: FYB.00097 © VTM, used under CC BY-SA. Source: digitaltmuseum.org; NF.1992-2038 © Haakon Michael Harriss / NFM, used under CC BY-SA. Source: digitaltmuseum.org; NF.1992-2038 © Haakon Michael Harriss / NFM, used under CC BY-SA. Source: digitaltmuseum.org; FYB.00097 © VTM, used under CC BY-SA. Source: digitaltmuseum.org.

P17: NF.1955-0492 © YS, permission of NFM; NF.1968-0637 © YS, permission of NFM; NF.1968-0637 © YS, permission of NFM; LB.06130 © VTM, used under CC BY-SA. Source: digitaltmuseum.org; FYB.00100 © VTM, used under CC BY-SA. Source: digitaltmuseum.org; FYB.00100 © VTM, used under CC BY-SA. Source: digitaltmuseum.org; FYB.00096 © VTM, used under CC BY-SA. Source: digitaltmuseum.org; NF.1949-0525 © Haakon Michael Harriss / NFM, used under CC BY-SA. Source: digitaltmuseum.org; NF.1955-0492 © YS, permission of NFM; NF.1911-1264 © Haakon Michael Harriss / NFM, used under CC BY-SA. Source: digitaltmuseum.org.

P18: NF.1992-2156 © YS, permission of NFM; BUM.0754 © YS, permission of HVM; HFU.17926 © YS, permission of HVM; HFU.00052 © YS, permission of HVM; BUM.1059 © YS, permission of HVM; BUM.1008 © YS, permission of HVM; © YS, permission of HVM; HFU.00028 © YS, permission of HVM; BG.00251 © YS, permission of HVM; BUM.1070 © YS, permission of HVM.

P19: NF.1897-0564 © YS, permission of NFM; NF.1911-0931 © YS, permission of NFM; NF.1992-1624 © Anne-Lise Reinsfelt / NFM, used under CC BY-SA. Source: digitaltmuseum.org; KBM.B.151 © HVM, used by permission; detail of NF.1897-0564 © YS, permission of NFM; detail of NF.1911-0931 © YS, permission of NFM; © YS, permission of HVM.

P20: Bunader fra Voss. Fra privatarkivet etter Gunnvor Ingstad Trætteberg. Used under CC-BY. Source: foto.digitalarkivet.no. Filename: 8508748955.jpg; NF.1992-1542 © YS, permission of NFM; NF.1992-1542 © NFM, used under CC BY-SA. Source: digitaltmuseum.org.

P21: NF.1895-1152 © YS, permission of NFM; NF.1895-1152 © YS, permission of NFM; © YS, permission of HVM; BUM.1154 © YS, permission of HVM; HFU.00209 © YS, permission of HVM.

P22: HFU.17926 © YS, permission of HVM; TGM-BM.1913:411 © YS, permission of TM; TGM-BM.1930-31:061 © YS, permission of TM; NF.1955-0305C © YS, permission of NFM; NF.1911-0474 © Anne-Lise Reinsfelt / NFM, used under CC BY-SA. Source: digitaltmuseum.org; TGM-BM.1915:098 © YS, permission of TM; TGM-BM.1930-31:061 © YS, permission of TM; NF.1899-0171 © YS, permission of NFM; NF.2000-0605 © Anne-Lise Reinsfelt / NFM, used under CC BY-SA. Source: digitaltmuseum.org; NF.2001-0067A © Anne-Lise Reinsfelt / NFM, used under CC BY-SA. Source: digitaltmuseum.org; BG.00251 © YS, permission of HVM; HFU.18368 © YS, permission of HVM; NF.1949-0545 © Haakon Michael Harriss / NFM, used under CC BY-SA. Source: digitaltmuseum.org; NF.1955-0492 © YS, permission of NFM; BUM.2047 © YS, permission of HVM; NF.1897-0564 © YS, permission of NFM; TGM-BM.1913:413 © YS, permission of TM; TGM-BM.1983:158 © YS, permission of TM; TGM-BM.1915 © YS, permission of TM; TGM-SM.2540 © YS, permission of TM; TGM-SM.2540 © YS, permission of TM; TGM-SM.2540 © YS, permission of TM; TGM-SM.2540 © YS, permission of NFM; NF.1955-0305C © YS, permission of NFM; NF.1992-2457 © Anne-Lise Reinsfelt / NFM, used under CC BY-SA. Source: digitaltmuseum.org; NF.1992-2484 © Anne-Lise Reinsfelt / NFM, used under CC BY-SA. Source: digitaltmuseum.org.

P23: TGM-SM.0711 © YS, permission of TM; NF.1912-0338 © Anne-Lise Reinsfelt / NFM, used under CC BY-SA. Source: digitaltmuseum.org; NF.1904-0181 © Anne-Lise Reinsfelt / NFM, used under CC BY-SA. Source: digitaltmuseum.org; NF.1913-1298; NF.1912-0345 © Anne-Lise Reinsfelt / NFM, used under CC BY-SA. Source: digitaltmuseum.org; NF.1992-2569 © Anne-Lise Reinsfelt / NFM, used under CC BY-SA. Source: digitaltmuseum.org; TGM-SM.2542 © YS, permission of TM; TGM-SM.0890 © YS, permission of TM; TGM-BM.1933-34:048 © YS, permission of TM; TGM-SM.0722 © YS, permission of TM; TGM-SM.0721 © YS, permission of TM; NF.1912-0489 © Anne-Lise Reinsfelt / NFM, used under CC BY-SA. Source: digitaltmuseum.org; NF.1910-0987 © Anne-Lise Reinsfelt / NFM, used under CC BY-SA. Source: digitaltmuseum.org; NF.1992-2485 © Anne-Lise Reinsfelt / NFM, used under CC BY-SA. Source: digitaltmuseum.org; NF.1992-2484 © Anne-Lise Reinsfelt / NFM, used under CC BY-SA. Source: digitaltmuseum.org; TGM-SM.0876 © YS, permission of TM; TGM-SM.0716 © YS, permission of TM; TGM-SM.0719 © YS, permission of TM; TGM-SM.0715 © YS, permission of TM; TGM-SM.0712 © YS, permission of TM.

P25: NF.1955-0305C © YS, permission of NFM; NF.2000-0162 © YS, permission of NFM; © Frode Inge Helland, used under CC BY-SA 3.0. Source: commons.wikimedia.org. Filename: 2010_10_20_Gulen_Mjømna_025.jpg

P26: TGM-SM.3131 © YS, permission of TM; TGM-SM.3131 © YS, permission of TM; based on TGM-SM.3131 © YS, permission of TM; NF.1968-0637 © YS, permission of NFM; NF.1992-2038 © Haakon Michael Harriss / NFM, used under CC BY-SA. Source: digitaltmuseum.org.

P67: NF.1899-0171 © YS, permission of NFM.

P90: TGM-BM.1915:103 © YS, permission of TM; TGM-SM.0891 © YS, permission of TM; TGM-SM.1545 © YS, permission of TM.

P91: TGM-BM.1915:103 © YS, permission of TM; TGM-SM.0891 © YS, permission of TM; TGM-SM.1545 © YS, permission of TM.

103

index

apron 6, 11, 13, 21
åttebladrose 11, 22, 88
Aust-Agder 6, 7, 8, 19, 52
Aust-Telemark 6, 14, 21, 47
baby wrap 6, 19, 43, 52
backstitch 95, 97
  turn 44, 69, 70, 77, 78
band sampler 36–43, 92
bag 28–29
bars 94, 96
basting *see tacking*
base layer 68, 74, 75, 76, 82, 83, 88, 89
belt, belte 13, 21, 24, 37, 42
boo boo stick 92
bookmark 44–45
breast cloth 18, 24
bringeduk 18
bringklut 18
brudgomaduk 15
brystduk 6, 18
brystklut 18
bunad 5, 6, 8, 9, 11, 21, 26
cap 6, 8, 17–18, 19, 39
changing threads 68, 76
chenille needle 26, 62, 74, 82, 88, 89, 100
chi monogram 22
collar 6, 7, 8, 9–11, 26, 28, 38, 39, 40, 41, 42, 43, 56, 67, 90, 91, 94, 95, 96, 97
coloured smøyg 5, 6, 8
compatibility, thread 100–102
corner, mitred 99
cotton
  fabric 9, 11, 16, 18, 24
  thread 9, 11, 13, 21, 25, 26
count, thread 10, 11, 13, 14, 18, 24, 25
counted tacking 66
cross 15, 19, 22
  hakekross 19, 22
  kinnekross 19, 22
  stitch 12, 14, 15, 19, 20, 21, 25
cuff 6, 7, 9, 10, 11, 21, 40
cushion 52–55
dåpslue 16–17
determining thread count 25
drawn thread 9, 94, 96
dreglehuve 16
dye 9, 16, 18, 26, 36, 73, 81
edging 67, 93, 94, 95, 96, 97
eldjarnrose 11, 22
embroidery hoop 67, 69, 76
error 92
essesaum 22
espresso pendant 35
evenweave 24, 25
fabric
  cotton 9, 11, 16, 18, 24
  count 10, 11, 13, 14, 18, 24, 25
  lacing 98
  linen 8, 9, 10, 11, 12, 13, 14, 15, 16, 18, 19, 24
  weave 24, 69, 71, 72, 77, 79, 80
finishing threads 73, 75, 81, 83
flat silk 25, 84, 86
flax 24
forerme 21
forklebord 11, 21
framed square 60–61
frame 67, 84, 86, 95, 97
front border turn 72, 80
handaplagg 6, 12
handkerchief 6, 15
hanging ornament 46
Hardanger 6, 8, 9, 11, 13, 15, 18, 21, 24, 25
headdress 20, 21
hem 99
holbeinsaum, holbeinsøm 14, 21, 25
holbein stitch 14, 15, 20
hoop 67, 69, 76
Hordaland 6, 7, 8, 19, 22, 25
hyllik 19
hylk 19
jewellery bag 28–29
kasteplagg 21
kinnlag 19
kinnplagg 19
kogin 7
kvarde 9
kvalesaum 67, 95, 97
lacing fabric 98
layer 8, 10, 67, 95, 97
  base 8, 26, 68, 74, 75, 76, 82, 83, 88, 89
  top 8, 26, 74, 75, 82, 83, 88, 89
laying tool 67, 84–85
left-handed 66
likkross 6, 14
linen 8, 9, 10, 11, 12, 13, 14, 15, 16, 18, 19, 24
lue 16–17, 19
luve 16–17
Mamluk 7
mænder-ruter 22
mistake 92
mitred corner 99
monochrome smøyg 5, 6
motif 5, 11, 12, 14, 15, 16, 19, 21, 22, 25
mouse tags 94, 96
multiple strands 67, 84, 85, 86, 87
needle 26, 62, 67, 74, 82, 88, 89, 100
needlebook 62
needlecase 30–31
new thread 68, 73, 76, 81
nyzynka 7
ornament 46
parked thread 73, 81
pendant 35, 51
plattsøm 9
poppy pendant 51
prewash 24
red with highlights smøyg 5
right-handed 66
Rogaland 7
row ends 44, 69–72, 73, 74, 77–80, 81, 82
runner 32–34
running stitch 5, 7, 8, 12, 26, 67, 68–75, 76–83, 88, 89
sampler 7, 36–43, 92
satin stitch 8, 9, 88, 89, 90, 91
scissor keep 62–64
scooping 67
Setesdal 6, 8, 16, 19, 52
sewing 67
sheep 21, 25–26
ship 22
shirt 6, 7, 8, 9–11, 18, 24, 26, 56–59
shrinkage 24
silk 7, 8, 9, 11, 12, 13, 14, 15, 19, 20, 21, 24, 25, 26, 84, 86, 92
silksaum 25
simple turn 69, 70, 77, 78
skaut 20
skjorte 9–11
slubs 24
Sogn og Fjordane 7
spælsau 21, 25–26
spissruter 22
square, framed 60–61
stabbing 67
starting 68, 69, 74, 76, 77, 82, 92
stem stitch 90, 91
stepped turn 71, 79
stitch
  cross 12, 14, 15, 19, 20, 21, 25
  holbein 14, 15, 20
  running 5, 7, 8, 12, 26, 67, 68–75, 76–83, 88, 89
  satin 8, 9, 88, 89, 90, 91
  stem 90, 91
  undoing 92
stitching paths 92
striped smøyg 5, 6, 15
svartsaum 6, 20, 25
table centre 47–50
table runner 32–34
tacking 66
tapestry needle 26, 62, 74, 82, 88, 89, 93, 100
tassel 15, 64
Telemark 5, 6, 7, 8, 9–10, 14, 15, 16, 21, 22, 24, 25, 26, 33, 38, 39, 40, 42, 43, 47, 94, 96
tension 67, 69, 70, 77, 78, 84, 85, 86, 87
thread
  changing 68, 76
  compatibility 100–102
  count 10, 11, 13, 14, 18, 24, 25
  finishing 73, 75, 81, 83
  length 25, 26
  parked 73, 81
  starting 68, 74, 76, 82
  withdrawing 92
tooth edging 28, 67, 93, 94, 95, 96, 97
top layer 8, 26, 74, 75, 82, 83, 88, 89
turn
  backstitch 44, 69, 70, 77, 78
  front border 72, 80
  simple 69, 70, 77, 78
  stepped 71, 79
valknute 22
vävsöm 7
Vest-Agder 7
Vest-Telemark 6, 16
ull 25–26
undoing stitches 92
vinterbunad 6, 11, 21
Voss 21, 25
warp 24, 25
weft 24, 25
wide stem stitch 90, 91
withdrawing threads 92
wool 25–26
woven bar 94, 95, 96, 97
yoke 6, 9, 11
zig-zag 11, 14, 18